TAKING CHARGE

GORDON N. McMINN
with
LARRY LIBBY

ACCENT BOOKS

Denver, Colorado

Third Printing 1981

ACCENT BOOKS
A division of Accent Publications, Inc.
12100 W. Sixth Avenue
P.O. Box 15337
Denver, Colorado 80215

Copyright © 1980 Accent Publications, Inc.
Printed in the United States of America

Library of Congress Catalog Card Number: 80-65061

ISBN 0-89636-043-1

88304

Contents

One Step Upstream

We were plunged midstream the moment we were born. Leaving behind the warm darkness of the womb we were unceremoniously shoved headlong into a rushing torrent of lights and smells and sounds. And we've been there ever since.

Life is a thing of movement; stop the movement and you stop the life. You never get out of the current; there is no such option. Yet, there is another option. Choice is that which makes us human—created in the image of God with attributes of intelligence, emotion and will. I may choose to simply allow the river to carry me along as it would, bouncing me from rock to rock, pulling inexorably downstream, or I may take charge. I may choose to resist the ceaseless, mindless, downward motion—to fight the current; to swim upstream.

Choice is our birthright, the essential statement of our humanness. Take away this decision-making power from man and you take away the man. That which gives evidence of life is a constant struggle against the backward tug.

Will your today be any different than your yesterday? Yes, on that you can depend. But how? Will you consciously participate in making the day worthwhile—different, better—than the last one? You can, you know. This book is designed to help you get started.

Are you discouraged? Perhaps you feel like a helpless branch rushed along in the chatter of the stream, bounced and bullied from circumstance to circumstance—swept along with little hope of forward motion or progress. You've tried one too many self-improvement schemes which didn't work. Your energies are gone and few seem to care or want to help.

Many different situations and experiences seem to be forcing you into the rapids. Trusted friends have let you down. The weight of responsibilities and duties pushes you under. The explosion of change creates swirling eddies of confusion and things highly valued glide by on the banks without providing the anchor and stability for which you crave. Moral decay, rising prices and shallow, transient relationships make you wonder who or what can be trusted.

"Hey, is this the way it's going to be?" you ask. "Am I going to spend my life tumbled along at the mercy and whim of chance and circumstance? Can't I ever get closer to the kind of person I really want to be?"

The Apostle Paul encourages us: "For if by the transgression of the one, death reigned through the one, much more those who receive the abundance of grace and of the gift of righteousness will reign in life through the One, Jesus Christ" (Romans 5:17).

Reign in life! That doesn't sound much like a helpless, hopeless forced march downstream, does it? To reign in life is to enjoy it supremely, conquer circumstances and forge forward into new and deeper channels of growth and improvement.

In the pages that follow, you will not be offered easy remedies for the troubles and pressures of life. Life *is* pressure—the water will continue to flow. Nor will you be offered a jet-boat ride up the rapids. Instead, you will learn something of the nature of the stream. You will find a method by which you may begin to take charge by taking that vital first step toward conscious growth. A shaky step perhaps, but a step against the current—one step upstream.

PART ONE
The Upstream Choice

If Job could have selected his own future, his livestock might have been spared from the raiding Sabeans, his children might have been rescued from disaster, and his body might have remained unravaged by disease. But the man from Uz was offered no such selection. Circumstance broke down the gates and burst into his life like an invading army. But Job still had a choice. He could choose how to respond.

If Paul and Silas could have been allowed their choice of overnight lodgings in downtown Philippi, they probably would not have decided on the prison. Or the inner dungeon. Or the stocks. Or the severe beating. But nobody asked the first-century missionaries their preference. Circumstance inhibited them, imprisoned them, enchained them. They couldn't move, couldn't struggle free, couldn't rise to their own defense. But Paul and Silas were free to make an all-important choice. They could choose how to respond. Because of their choice, their dungeon echoed with song.

No matter how yesterday haunts you, how today pressures you, how tomorrow frightens you—you too have a choice. Circumstance can never take the power of choice away from you. You cannot predict your circumstances, you cannot know your future, but you can choose your response to what each day brings into your life. That difference might make a choir loft out of a dungeon.

1
The Right To Choose My Destiny

With a voice as cool as iced tea, Pat openly described to me her freedom to have sex with several young men.

"It's not like I'm a slut or something," she maintained. She wouldn't go to bed with just *any* man. Then again, neither would she hesitate if she felt particularly attached to someone. Pat seemed to disdain the gossip as well as the reputation she had gained in her high school.

That was before the inevitable happened. Pat became pregnant. Leaving school and gossip behind, she went to another state to have the baby.

Over a year later, Pat wrote me a letter. The cool, worldly airs were gone. Out of the letter poured feelings of guilt and despair from a broken girl who found that what she thought was freedom was something else. Something like a trap. Her decision to engage in casual sex with several men was wrong. The myth of "free love" evaporated as the snare of reality jerked her from school before graduation and thrust upon her the responsibilities of an unwed mother.

What is freedom? What does it mean to be totally free? If freedom is to have any value at all, it must live within definitive borders. We are free to do right; we are free to live justly. When rules are broken, freedom is engulfed by circumstance like water over a crumbled seawall until justice takes over to enforce the rules and rebuild the dikes.

A person who is free lives an ordered life within the limits of a well-defined conscience. The perimeters of freedom are bounded by the collective conscience or rules of any defined group within which I may live. I am a free citizen of the United States. Free, that is, within the boundaries of constitutional rights, the laws of the United States, the statutes of the state in which I live, the ordinances of my county, and the varied cluster of mutual understandings with a half-dozen of my neighbors.

And you might add a whole kaleidoscope of other crisscrossing rules and borders if you happen to subscribe to the respective codes of the Kiwanis Club, the Baptist church, the local PTA, or a Monday morning carpool. Boil all that down and you arrive at the final self-established standard of freedom—your own conscience. Within your own conscience, within God's immutable laws and within the confines of the authority structure in which you live, you are free.

"Great," you reply, "free to do what?" You are free to choose, to take charge of the decision-making process. When you decide to violate the rules of your own conscience or of those authoritative bodies to which you must submit, you are deciding against freedom. When Pat went looking for sexual liberties, she unwittingly checked into a prison camp. You may decide to shun what is right, but that isn't freedom. If your decision is repeated until it becomes a habitual thing, the result may be slavery.

You go to the doctor for a physical. Tests indicate that your blood sugar level is borderline. To improve your health, you are sternly warned to cut down on your intake of sweets, to eat fewer things with sugar in them. But you have an incurable fascination for Smacko candy bars. In spite of the doctor's recommendation, you decide to eat at least one Smacko every day. Though you were free to decide, you have not acted freely. The consequences of your self-destructive behavior could lead to an ultimate diagnosis of crippling diabetes.

Deciding on those activities which enhance your life will lead to a feeling of productivity and freedom. Deciding on those activities which violate the rules of your own conscience or the codes of the society in which you live is like setting a time bomb. If the guilt doesn't explode right away, it will surely drain all your energies as you wait for that moment to occur.

Making a decision to act can lead to a rewarding feeling of growth, but it can also lead to the burning feeling of failure. A decision can brighten the day with its reward when it leads to success, or dampen the joy with its disappointment when it doesn't work out as planned. Each decision carries with it a risk: will the decision lead to a happy experience or a painful one?

Mike wants to ask vivacious Evie for a date. On the one hand he weighs the bliss of an evening with this dynamite damsel, and on the other hand he considers the possible sting of rejection if she says, "No, thank you." To put off picking up the phone is to put off the apprehension of such a moment, but it may also mean that someone else may slip a ring on Evie's left hand and that would be that.

To avoid pain it might seem wiser to avoid decisions. But what happens when you choose not to decide? You don't make mistakes that way, so you don't get hurt. But then, you don't grow either. Constructive alternatives to living only result when you risk choosing to decide.

Your car is six years old. Several parts have had to be replaced lately. Major repairs will be needed within a year. Should you buy another car? You begin by asking several questions: "What alternatives are there? How much money would it take? What kind of car would I want? When is the best time to get another car?"

As you toss the questions around in your mind you come to a barrier. Rather than working your way over or around this difficulty you turn your thoughts to something else and fail to make a decision.

As you procrastinate, the car throws a piston and your alternatives are pruned severely. By choosing not to decide, you have allowed circumstance to dictate your decision. You have surrendered your options to chance.

What is the right thing to do? When confronted with a

difficult situation, you need to think through the questions carefully, gain the information needed, then decide on a course of action. You plan what you will do. It may or may not work out well, but you have made a decision. Since it is your decision, you have a sense of responsibility for what happens. You are rewarded with the decision when it is a good one and you learn when the decision sinks like an anvil on a lilypad. You have exercised your right to choose your own destiny. Here is where growth begins, with an internal decision—an act of the will that is determined by the individual, not by the dictates of circumstance.

Life, like an internal kettle, often simmers with certain stresses and frustrations. If the frustration is minor, we let it simmer, hoping it will go away. If the stress is too great, however, and the kettle begins to boil over, we may be so overwhelmed that we are unable to make any decisions.

Stress is neither good nor bad. It is a consequence of living in a dynamic, changing world. An inevitable part of life. But how we choose to *respond* to that stress is all-important. Simply ignoring the situation can breed a dangerous insensitivity. It happens like this:

In order to protect our emotions, we avoid stressful subjects and choose not to make decisions. Barring the front door to these persistent frustrations succeeds only in driving them to the back door. The intruders return in the form of such destructive moods as guilt, fear, or bitterness. Unresolved, these feelings feed on life's delicate tissues like a cancer and keep us from productive living.

A carpenter need not react to every little splinter in his hand. If he did, he would spend all of his time pulling out tiny slivers instead of building. However, you would expect the carpenter to react if he cut himself quite badly while sawing a board. If he did not, but repeatedly ignored such cuts pretending they hadn't happened, it would most likely reflect in the quality of his work. He would tend to become sloppy and careless. If not attended to, his insensitivity to physical pain, to the irritation of being hurt would tend to make the carpenter insensitive in other areas as well. If he wasn't worried about a nail in his foot, chances are he wouldn't be overly concerned about *any* of the nails—halfway in, halfway out or sprinkled all over the driveway. That carpenter must determine an appropriate level of response to physical discomfort.

At what point should you be sensitive to irritations? Like the carpenter, you cannot afford to let every little frustration trigger a response. If you did, you would spend your life reacting rather than acting. You must determine at what level of frustration an appropriate response should be triggered.

How then should you respond to those deeper cuts—those periods of intense stress or grief?

Larry's dad is a pastor. For more than twenty years this pastor has helped people work through their feelings in stressful situations. Recently he had to face his own moment of truth.

Larry had gone to a youth retreat. He jumped into the canoe. The lake was calm as he paddled for an arm of the other shore. In what must have seemed like the briefest instant, one of those freak winds that comes up so quickly and dies down in ten minutes tore at the surface of the lake with careless fury. Eight weeks later the body had not been found.

How does the pastor respond? For eighteen years he and his wife have invested in the life of their son. Can they close the book in sixty seconds? "Why did God choose our son? Why at this time when he had so much to offer? He was such a fine young man."

As the storm of pain rages, it would be easy for the pastor and his wife to hide from their feelings behind great heavy doors. The tide of guilt and fear and bitterness is so savage and the doubts concerning the goodness of God are so troubling it only seems natural to lock these feelings away in a deep inner closet. But to do so will accomplish no good. Time is needed to work on the grief, to appreciate and affirm the value of Larry's life, and to resolve the feel-ings toward his death. Some questions may never be answered. They need not be. God is just. He always does what is right. His love is as constant as the morning sunrise.

> These things I have spoken to you, that in Me you may have peace. In the world you have tribulation [pressure], but take courage; I have overcome the world (John 16:33).

A literal reading could be, "...In this world you will be squeezed by pressure..." You will have stress. Forces will push and pull you in this ocean of motion, the constant flux of life. You do not escape from the stresses of life when you become a Christian. But you are joined to the One who has overcome.

In II Corinthians 4:8 and 9, the Apostle Paul tells us that we may be pressed by troubles on every side, but that's not going to crush us. We may be perplexed when we don't know why things happen as they do, but we don't get discouraged and quit.

Stress is not a trial or testing imposed on us by God. It is broader than that. True, God brings circumstances into our lives to enable us to grow. But to view every stress as a trial, testing or temptation would not be valid.

If, for instance, we fail to eat for a period of time certain stress will be created when we have not treated our body in the habitual manner to which it is accustomed. There will be emotional consequences as well. We may find that we become easily annoyed or irritable at minor incidents when we are hungry. This is not a testing. It is due to the fact that we have not eaten. Stress is an inevitable consequence of living.

You may ask, "Isn't God in control of all matters in life? Isn't God sovereign?" Certainly, God who created all things, if He is God, has all knowledge and all power. He sees everything that happens. The Bible says that not a sparrow falls but God knows. He is such a God of detail that even the hairs of our head are numbered.

Yet this God who knows all and sees all and has all power has given His children the right to choose, to make decisions. The stakes are awesome, for man may choose to reject God forever and spend an eternity banished from His presence.

"Doesn't God care?" you ask. "How could He allow people to make that terrible choice?"

The entrance of Jesus into the dirt, sweat and tears of our planet has answered that doubt forever. God *does* care and has gone the limit in demonstrating that care, but He will not *force* a choice on anyone. The Bible sets forth many alternatives and the consequences of those alternatives are also recorded. One path leads to a life of abundance and deep joy. Other roads lead to despair. You have the right to choose your own destiny.

As Joshua approached the end of a long life as the leader of God's chosen people, he set down alternatives for the generation which followed. Gathering the last vestiges of his own great strength, the old general called all the masses of Israel together to hear his farewell address:

> Now, therefore, fear the Lord and serve Him in sincerity and truth; and put away the gods which your fathers served beyond the River and in Egypt, and serve the Lord. And if it is disagreeable in your sight to serve the Lord, choose for yourselves today whom you will serve: whether the gods which your fathers served which were beyond the River, or the gods of the Amorites in whose land you are living; but as for me and my house, we will serve the Lord (Joshua 24: 14-15).

It really wasn't much of a choice at all. Any school kid could have weighed the benefits of serving lifeless, powerless images of wood and stone against serving Yahweh, Deliverer of Israel, the living God. Why should anyone with a teaspoon of sanity choose the gods of their enemies over the God of their fathers? Why should anyone opt for impotence over power, death over life, hell over heaven? Strange that such a selection should even be offered.

Nevertheless, Israel will never be able to stand before God and declare that she had no choice in the matter. None of us will.

INTERACTION #1

Determine an area of personal need in each of the following areas. Express that need in terms of a goal you would like to see achieved.

_____ SOCIAL:

_____ FAMILY:

_____ SPIRITUAL:

_____ OCCUPATIONAL:

_____ PERSONAL:

Now, rank these needs in order of urgency, numbering

them one through five.

As you read on in this book, keep a journal with a page for each of the above needs. As you reflect on them, write down what will need to be done in order to achieve each of your goals. What excuses and hindrances will you need to overcome? Get them down on paper.

2
Responding to Stress: Capitulation

Have you noticed how busy life is lately? So many things to do and so little time to get them done. Perhaps you feel like the person who said when he had time he was going to have a nervous breakdown. He had worked hard for it and no one was going to take it away from him.

Did you ever catch bees in a jar on one of those barefoot August afternoons of your childhood? Bouncing from clover blossom to dandelion (then back to the blossom just in case he'd missed something), the meticulous creature toils in the sunshine, unaware of the Mason jar descending over his landscape. Got him! Oh, is he mad!

To snare another one you have to be quick as a frog's tongue, opening and closing the lid so as not to release the prisoner's wrathful cell mate. The captive army makes the jar hum like a transformer until it feels as though it will explode. The more bees the more buzz, as they claw for an opening, crawl over each other, careen against the lid and crave an opportunity to sting some kid on the nose.

Can you imagine that jar inside of yourself?

A certain stressful situation intrudes into your busy schedule. You open your jar for an instant, insert the unhappy creature, quickly screw the lid down again. The stress keeps bouncing around in the jar. You feel it moving in there, but it's muted—muffled—and the lid is on tight so it can't get out. As other stresses come along, you pry open the lid just wide enough to put them in the jar, then firmly secure the lid to keep everything inside. Soon you have a jar full of pulsating, active creatures bounding against the glass, thumping the jar lid, cascading against one another. It's a wonder the jar doesn't explode. In fact it may. Feelings are to be acted upon, not bottled up. No one can live productively when stinging things are hurling themselves against the inner human walls trying to get out.

A few years ago, I found the pace of life extremely demanding. It seemed increasingly impossible to get caught up on my work. The pile left on my desk at the end of the day seemed to reproduce itself overnight so as to look even more formidable by morning. It actually seemed like the harder I worked, the further I fell behind. My wife, Donna, had gone back to school. With the children off to college she was able to go to work as an elementary school teacher.

It wasn't that life didn't seem productive—it certainly was. But there was an overriding sense of frustration. To maintain my position with the seminary, relate with the children, enjoy my wife and home, and keep up with the social and religious activities to which I was committed created a high degree of stress. Sometimes there was so much to be accomplished on a given day that I couldn't get anything done at all. I found myself staring stupidly at the same sentence on a report for ten minutes.

When this sort of behavior began to manifest itself, I found it absolutely essential to break away for awhile. After a few hours to relax, to enjoy life, to smell the flowers if you will, I was ready to begin scaling the mountain of work on my desk once again. (Amazing how it looked a little lower in elevation!) Renewed in energy, I found my efforts were far more productive than when I had left the work.

Have you spent time thinking of all you have to do and, as a result, got nothing done? After several hours you think, "Good night, now I'm even further behind than before! I've wasted all this time worrying about my work instead of catching up."

Such feelings are not unusual. When the schedule of activities gets too busy, it creates frustration within us. We feel like an outlet into which ten extension cords have been plugged. There are so many activities operating from that one outlet—so many things to do—that we can't possibly get them all done. We feel a loss of drive to work on the task immediately before us. Although we know it has to be done, it is only one of several thousand others. It seems impossible to get started; we keep putting it off. As a result, we are not as productive as we would like to be and that increases our frustration overload even further. The outlet's getting hot. One of these days it'll blow a fuse right out of the socket.

DIAGRAM ONE

CAPITULATION (A)

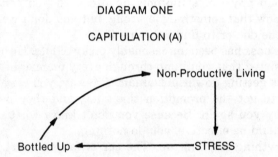

Non-Productive Living

Bottled Up ◀—————————STRESS

When you feel bombarded by many decisions and don't know where to get started, it often results in that tired feeling or loss of drive.

As a result, you spend valuable time getting little done which makes you feel worse, for now you have more to do and less time to get it accomplished.

Such a response pattern spirals like the snowball in the cartoon—plummeting down the mountain, picking up more snow and speed as it races to the bottom of the slope. The more we bottle up our frustration resulting from the inability to accomplish all that needs to be done, the more we lose drive, the more non-productive we become, the greater the frustration that needs to be bottled up . . . and on rolls the snowball—right toward the edge.

23

The only way to break this self-defeating circle is through a change of pace. Let some of the bees out of the jar. Take the lid off. Take a walk. Relax for awhile, even if only for a short time. When you return to your activities you will find that you are not only refreshed, but more productive as well. A fresh start oftentimes supplies a fresh approach and gets one off the dead-end street and back on the freeway.

When we feel incapable of meeting the multiple demands of a given day we sense that helpless feeling of stress welling up inside.

Certain physical symptoms have caused you concern. You know that something is wrong, but you don't want to go to the doctor to find out what it is.

Your boss has been unreasonably picky of late. He or she has insisted that you jump through every manner of hoop and it's getting downright unfair. Anyway, you were supposed to get the promotion this time, and they passed right by you again. Because you don't know what to do that would be effective, you do nothing.

Everything is piling up. The car is falling apart. The power company sent you that coldly polite second notice. Your mate has been sick and really needs to go to the doctor again. One kid is in trouble at school for fighting and the other one has certainly been quiet lately—too quiet. All the toast seems to be popping up at once, and you don't know what to do.

Begin with the first step. Select one area of frustration and develop a plan for action. The current in the stream may be raging, but you can still take one step upstream.

Frustration builds when things don't go as planned. Sue found a young man in her English class to be particularly attractive. During every afternoon study hall she planned her approach. Without appearing too aggressive she would try to be friendly and open. Maybe he would ask her out—he didn't seem to have a steady girl. Up in her room one evening, she heard the phone ring downstairs.

"It's for you, Sue," her dad called up. It was Tom! Was he going to ask her out tonight? There were lots of things going on at school that week. A game, a concert, the play—she'd really been wanting to see the play.

"Hey Sue, I was wondering if you had Vicky's phone number—can't find it anywhere."

"It's unlisted."

"Oh, yeah? No wonder. Got it handy?"

"Yeah."

"Hey, whaddya think—she's your friend. Do you think she'd go out with me? Do you think she'd want to go to the play?"

"Probably."

"Oh, wow! Here goes nothin'. What was that number?"

Sue managed to come up with the phone number and finish the conversation without letting Tom know how he had just devastated her week. Tears were in her eyes as she went down to the kitchen looking for a way to compensate for the big empty place she felt inside. That chocolate cake she had made last night looked good. She sliced a big piece, wolfed it down and cut another.

As Sue encountered other frustrations from her anticipation for dates in the weeks that followed, she found that she was spending a good deal more time in the kitchen. She baked and consumed more and more cakes, gaining weight until she began to look like a big round cake herself. The heavier she became, the less attention she received from the boys she was hoping would ask her out. The more she was ignored, the more she tried to resolve her frustration by eating.

The snowball was gaining momentum. As it moved toward the bottom of the hill, Sue became increasingly depressed. She questioned her worth. No one liked her, she thought. Not really. There were days when she thought about death and how much easier it would be if . . .

What pushed Sue into these feelings of deep depression where she questioned the value of her own life? Was it not due to the stress that was bottled up in that inner jar of hers?

To compensate for the emptiness Sue felt, she indulged in self-destructive eating patterns. The more weight she gained, the worse she felt about herself, for she realized that the weight was hurting her, not helping her. Yet she seemed helpless to do anything about her situation, to stop the pattern of self-defeating behavior. It made her disgusted to look in a mirror—and the more disgusted she became the more depressed she was and the more she doubted her worth.

DIAGRAM TWO

CAPITULATION (B)

Bottled Up ◄——————— STRESS

Restlessness or
Boredom

Immediate Gratification
of Needs

Depression

If things don't go the way you had planned, it can be very agitating. After this has happened numerous times, you learn ways to get rid of your feelings of irritation.

The methods you choose may not be good for you. When you choose to calm upset feelings by engaging in actions that are self-destructive, it will bring on feelings of depression.

Andy's parents repeatedly told their only son how much they expected from him. He could go to any university he chose and they would pay the bill. Both of his parents were graduates cum laude from elite colleges and were now launched in successful careers. Could any less be expected from their son? No one in the family seemed overly concerned that Andy's grade point average was 1.5 on a 4.0 scale at the end of his junior year. Even the state schools required a minimum of 2.0 unless you had high scores on your college entrance examinations. But a state school would never do for Andy. His parents were looking at the more prestigious big-name universities.

That was in the future, but just now Andy seemd to be barely tolerating school at all. He couldn't wait until the last bell of the day rang and he could take off in his car. Weekends were always the same: Friday and Saturday night, Andy would buy enough beer to get thoroughly drunk. He would drink the beer as quickly as he could until he passed out. Usually, he drank alone. When he regained consciousness, he would get into his car and take to the backroads at reckless high speeds. He drove alone also for he admitted that he didn't want to hurt anyone else.

His parents' expectations were just too high; he couldn't possibly live up to their standard. He had been a big disappointment to them for as long as he could remember. So why even try? Not knowing how to deal with the frustration that seethed like an acid inside, Andy started his pattern of problem drinking. He knew that his behavior was self-destructive—he knew the fuse was burning dangerously close to the powder—but it seemed like his only hope of escape from the pressures and the boredom of school.

What causes depression? There may be many causes of which we are not aware. One cause is engaging in self-defeating behavior which makes you feel devalued. You say, "If I thought more of myself, I wouldn't treat myself that way."

You feel guilty. We are not talking about a neurotic guilt which is based on faulty thinking or compulsive standards. This can seldom be ameliorated by asking for forgiveness. We want to zero in on that inhibitory feeling of guilt which comes when stress is bottled up.

It is vital to be able to distinguish the difference between a healthy regret over wrongdoing and an unhealthy debilitating feeling of guilt. The conscience serves as an inner policeman, blowing the whistle when you have done wrong. When such notice is served, you realize that you are guilty of wrongdoing, and you seek to make restitution, to re-establish a right relationship with the one who has been wronged.

Have you ever thought: "My wrong is too great; my sin is too deep. This time I cannot be forgiven; my guilt remains"?

David expressed a similar sentiment:

> For evils beyond number have surrounded me; My iniquities have overtaken me, so that I am not able to see; They are more numerous than the hairs of my head; And my heart has failed me (Psalm 40:12).

Feelings of guilt that come from wrongdoing get locked inside when we are unable or unwilling to accept forgiveness from another. Feelings of bitterness or resentment get locked up when we are unable or unwilling to forgive another person who has wronged us. Bottled together in a pressurized inner jar, the unhealthy mixture boils and fumes and eats at the fabric of our sense of well-being. Guilt feelings make us reluctant to try anything new, for we do not want to do greater wrong. The desire to take charge, to move upstream, is severely crippled.

Linda's situation perplexed the counselor. All test scores indicated a high level of ability; yet, her grades were below average. Her parents seemed to demonstrate a high degree of love and concern for Linda. Brothers and sisters before her had performed commendably. What was wrong?

Linda's performance could not be understood apart from a deeper look into her background. Adopted when she was nine, her previous home environment had been deporable. Shabbily dressed and often hungry or ill, Linda had been neglected and abused by her first parents. Finally the authorities had removed Linda from her home.

The atmosphere in her new home was entirely different. Her needs were lovingly cared for. For the first time in her life, she had nice new clothing to wear and healthy food was served at regularly scheduled mealtimes each day. Loving parents and brothers and sisters talked to her and seemed genuinely interested in her welfare.

What had she done to deserve all this kindness? She had come from an environment where she was punished and told that she was bad. Linda felt the response of love in her new home was not deserved. As a result, Linda was hounded by feelings of guilt. She could not do well in school for she did not feel she had the right to do well. Even in the happiest of family-together times she felt a sense of unworthiness that cast a shadow of guilt across her joy. All of the kindness and attention bestowed on her by her adopted family was boggling to the mind. The forgiveness offered to her in a new life and a new setting was more than she could understand or accept.

DIAGRAM THREE

CAPITULATION (C)

Feelings of guilt come from things you should have done and didn't. They also come from things you shouldn't have done, but did do. Such feelings can be useful as a guide for present and future activities.

When guilt feelings get bottled up instead of acted upon, it may result in feelings of depression.

The pathway out of depression is narrow, steep and often slippery. "Pull yourself together," is seldom said to one

29

who can.

Help does not come from that one who stands at the peak of the trail and shouts back, "Climb on out of there." Rather, it proceeds from those who meet that depressed person where he is and shows him a better way to move out of the canyon. It happens when a person you care about touches your life and says, "You're worth more than that. Get up and get going. Don't look back. Don't crawl back into that cave of despair. You owe it to yourself to forge ahead. There is a whole new perspective further on. Let's figure out a way to get there together."

Capitulation, or giving in to stress, is a destructive choice. We cannot grow when we allow these unresolved feelings to seethe and burn away at our inner self. And sooner or later, some of the angry stinging bees will find a way out of the jar—we won't be quite fast enough to screw down the lid. Often physical ailments, called psychosomatic illnesses, are a result. Ulcers, constipation, back problems, forms of asthma, certain allergies and a variety of respiratory diseases may be attributed to capitulation.

Catching bees in a jar does not make them go away. Although those particular captured bees may not be buzzing at my head, they are still very much alive, growing more vicious and vindictive by the moment in their captivity, watching for a weakness or opening in the jar so that they might rush out to afflict and cause pain. And there are always more bees—always more stressful situations that intrude into life and demand to be dealt with.

The answer is not to catch each frustration and hide it away inside to be faced at a more convenient hour; the answer is in learning to develop a plan to meet each stress head-on, to counter it with constructive action.

Suppressing our feelings leads only to an increased sense of frustration and the self-destructive downward spiral has begun. The snowflake becomes the snowball which becomes the avalanche.

How is it with you? Have you been hurting yourself by bottling up your feelings? Have you been unable to accept God's forgiveness? Perhaps you feel that you have gone too far, failed too often, or sinned too deeply to receive God's forgiveness. This is the lie our adversary, Satan, would have us believe.

DIAGRAM FOUR

CAPITULATION (A, B & C)

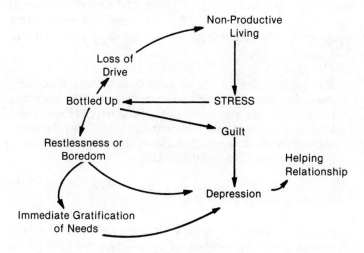

Capitulation in times of stress may result in: 1) a loss of drive which lowers your level of productivity; 2) feelings of irritation which lead you to engage in self-destructive acts and bring on depression: or 3) guilt feelings which lead to depression.

Stress which is bottled up can cause psychosomatic illnesses. Feelings locked inside tend to produce greater stress, like an enlarging spiral. Capitulation is not growth-producing.

The truth is, God does not look at us on the basis of what we've done or haven't done. No matter how good we've been, it's simply not good enough to meet God's standard of holy living.

Nor can we punish ourselves to win His approval. The punishment we deserve has already fallen on Jesus Christ. It does not depend on how good or how bad we have been, but on whether or not one has accepted God's freely-offered provision for forgiveness.

Jesus said, "... the one who comes to Me I will certainly not cast out" (John 6:37b).

It is not God's desire that we languish in guilt and spend our short lives in the grip of stress and despair. He longs for us to accept His love and forgiveness and move into a productive life that brings joy to our days and credit to His name.

> He has not dealt with us according to our sins, nor rewarded us according to our iniquities. For high as the heavens are above the earth, So great is His loving-kindness toward those who fear Him. As far as the east is from the west, So far has He removed our transgressions from us (Psalm 103:10-12).

> ... casting all your anxiety upon Him, because He cares for you (I Peter 5:7).

You *can* choose to keep all your cares and worries within yourself. Just remember if you do, the choice is yours ... not God's.

INTERACTION #2

One very practical way you can help other people is to listen when they have something bothering them. The object at this point is simply to try to reduce their bottled-up stress, not to solve the problem.

Consciously set aside some time to listen—really listen—to a friend. As you do, exercise the following precautions:

DON'T PUSH FOR INFORMATION. Let your friend tell you as much or as little as he wants to.

ALLOW AMPLE TIME. Be committed to hear him out—no backpedaling or glancing at your watch. Your friend will feel let down if you cut him off in the midst of relating his concern. So would you.

AVOID GIVING ANSWERS. It's tough, but try. Just listen for once. Try to rephrase what you are hearing and say it back to your friend.

THANK YOUR FRIEND FOR SHARING HIS CONCERN WITH YOU. Let him feel good about it, like he did the right thing by trusting you. It is a privilege reserved for friends.

3
Responding to Stress: Withdrawal

It is a brief pause. Just long enough for the sense of aloneness to catch up and swallow the woman alive. Bizarre, elongated shadows and a gathering breeze from the face of the mountain speak with one voice to that which the climber had already discerned. She won't make it—not today.

The peak whispers an invitation—so near, so near . . . . But the goal set early that morning must be surrendered. Turning her back on the mountain and a sky of wild crimson, she begins to pick her way through the loose shale back to that suitable campsite a half hour down the trail. The quest will be resumed in the morning when the aching body is renewed by a night's rest. A good meal and a fresh opportunity to study the maps will prepare the climber for tomorrow's feat. The mountain will be conquered, but not today.

It is wisdom for the climber to know her limitations. Others have lurched ahead, heedless of the dark and ill-prepared for the sudden storms of the night. Not all return. How foolish to go on when the chances to reach the goal are so slim. Still, there is reticence. Will she have another chance to make the climb? Will tomorrow's weather make another attempt impossible? Will she ever have another weekend—enough nerve—to dare the mountain alone?

Consider another mountain, another climber, on a different day. In many ways the setting was similar. A murky sky and cold twilight breeze called further progress into question. Fatigue kept shouting down that inner resolve to complete the climb and stand on the pinnacle. Looking at the clouds and then his watch, the climber decided to turn back to the safety of the camp a mile below. But this decision was different for he had come within a thousand feet of his goal. There would be no further opportunity. He gave up too soon.

Here is one of life's ultimate puzzles. There are times when just a little extended effort could achieve matchless results and worthy goals. At other times, it is just as necessary to recognize the waste and obscurity of pouring further energy into a task. You alone must make the decision whether to try to finish or to abandon the endeavor and begin another. You may be deemed a wise man or a fool, depending on the results of your decision.

When do you press the attack in the face of risk and ridicule? Perhaps no trail has been charted in the past and there are others who will follow your lead. Is it a moment to step out and torch the bridge behind you, or is it a moment to withdraw and quietly seek another avenue? It is never an easy question. The answer will be uniquely your own.

How many times had the pastor looked across his desk at a weeping man or woman in need of counsel. The irony touched his thoughts as he now wept in a counseling office. How many times had he leaned forward in his own chair to comfort a broken, sobbing individual who poured out his sorrow across the desk. Now it was his turn in a strange office, and the counselor put a hand on the pastor's heaving shoulders.

His ministry had been blown apart. He could never approach the pulpit again. And everything had been going so well. Church membership was climbing at last; he sensed a warm reception to his ministry. Many of the "fringe" members were swallowing their timidity and stepping into leadership roles. The logjam of indifference was giving way before a new current of optimism.

True, it had not been without cost. He could never remember working so hard—not even in seminary. It was troubling that his family climate had seemed overcast for weeks. His wife was a little aloof... perhaps it was because he had skipped several meals last week. And then there hadn't been much time to help with the kids, perhaps that was it. Would the congregation notice?

There were only these few, vague worries on the pastor's mind when his home and ministry were suddenly detonated in a violent domestic explosion which jarred every window in town. A member of his family had become involved in an adulterous affair. Word got around.

The pastor resigned. Searing gossip and criticism made the community unlivable. Wave after wave of shame engulfed the pastor and his wife until death seemed preferable to going on. Too late, he realized the depth of harm that had come from the neglect of his wife and children. Planting a flag on the peak of a mountain was not worth cutting the ropes and leaving his party to struggle and stumble on behind.

Growth comes out of failure as well as success. Having learned from his devastating fall, the pastor now leads a healed, united family. He is aware of his vulnerabilities. He knows that retreat does not always mean defeat—but, rather, the better part of wisdom.

Where do you invest your energies? How do you know when to accept a challenge and when to withdraw? It is easy to get so overextended that you cannot do anything well. It is also easy to become so timid that you shut out opportunities to expand your borders and conquer new territory.

The phone rang at 4:00 a.m. in our next-door neighbor's bedroom. The long distance operator had a collect call waiting from an unknown name in an unknown village of Scotland. The operator would allow the caller one word to state the nature of the call and, through the thousands of copper-wire miles, the strange voice uttered the perplexing word, "inheritance." To accept the call would mean a fifty dollar phone bill. To reject the call would mean a rejection of ... what? An ancestral castle rising out of a field of purple heather? A king's ransom in gold dubloons hoarded for a lifetime by an eccentric Scottish uncle? Or was it all a prank?

The operator's voice crackled again—would they accept the call? They would not. They hung up the phone, turned out the light and went back to bed. Was it the right time to withdraw? Or should they have accepted the risk, brushed aside their incredulity and found out what the mysterious call was all about? (They never did.)

You are faced by such decisions every day of your life, although lacking perhaps the dramatic quality of the preceding incident. You can consciously decide in what activities you will invest your energies. Similarly, you can choose to withdraw. When you fail to respond to stress by making a conscious choice, the decision will be governed by the habits you have developed in your lifetime.

Is the picture clear? You may choose to invest your energy and your resources in an activity or opportunity, you may choose to withdraw in that situation, or you may fail to make any choice and simply surrender to your pre-established habits.

Running your life by habit is like flying a plane on automatic pilot. Habits are necessary in our fast-paced culture because we are not able to consciously grapple with each decision in the great torrents of decisions that pour into our lives daily.

"Ah—there is a stop sign at that intersection. Now let me consider this. Should I put my foot on the brake or should I put off thinking this matter through until next Monday? Hmm."

Obviously, our minds could not endure a conscious mulling over of every action throughout the day. We might never make it to breakfast! Productive habits can provide convenient controls. Certain areas of our life can be switched onto automatic pilot while the conscious mind is free to explore other dimensions of living.

An experienced sailor may successfully pilot his one-man

craft in the wind through the water while at the same time visually surveying the distant shoreline. Does he have to furl his sails and throw out his anchor in order to take a moment to scan the horizon? Of course not. How could he ever make any progress? Routine patterns of behavior are not growth-producing in themselves, but they are nevertheless essential. There is value in having a road of past experience. You've been there before. You've tried this and it works. Next time the anxiety level goes up from a similar circumstance you'll know what to do. Every encounter with life does not need to be a new one.

One time, busily engaged in a task, I reached down and firmly gripped my soldering iron by the wrong end. I don't need to do that every time in order to discern the proper end for holding and the proper end for soldering. Once was ample. From past experiences you learn certain actions to avoid. You tried something and it didn't work out well. Next time you will do it differently.

Seventh-graders Bob and Jerry had a heated argument which resulted in a fight. Jerry, quicker and stronger than Bob, gained an immediate advantage and proceeded to press the point. Bob nursed his physical wounds for more than a week. He did not savor the idea of a return bout. The route which Bob normally walked to catch the school bus would take him right in front of his adversary's home. Upon a moment's reflection, Bob chose to seek an alternate route. Fearful of seeing Jerry again and getting into a second, painful battle, Bob chose a different bus stop in a different direction in order to avoid a confrontation.

Was this a wise decision for Bob? Perhaps it was. Aware of his lack of combative abilities, he chose to withdraw from a setting that created stress.

It is wise to be aware of your vulnerabilities. This same wisdom indicates when you should stand firm and when you should flee. In Genesis 39, the Bible tells of an incident in the life of Joseph. A certain Egyptian entrepreneur named Potiphar purchased Joseph as a slave after

Joseph's brothers ungraciously sold him to an Ishmaelite caravan. Joseph handled the situation rather well, however, and was soon placed in a position of authority in his master's household.

Potiphar's wife also noticed Joseph and used her wiles in order to entice him into having sex with her. Joseph politely but firmly declined. One day when they were alone in the house together, she became insistent and grabbed hold of his clothes. Joseph fled, leaving his garment in the hands of Potiphar's wife. Joseph realized this was neither the time nor place to discuss the matter with her. It was the moment to put shoe leather to his moral convictions and he did.

The Bible indicates that the believer needs to be keenly aware of his weaknesses and limitations. It is foolish to put yourself into situations where you know you will be hurt. Can you expect God to protect you from making a poor choice when you step deliberately into the path of a great temptation? Does an alcoholic taking the cure spend his time watching TV in the local tavern?

> Therefore let him who thinks he stands take heed lest he fall. No temptation has overtaken you but such as is common to man; and God is faithful, who will not allow you to be tempted beyond what you are able, but with the temptation will provide the way of escape also, that you may be able to endure it. Therefore, my beloved, flee from idolatry (I Corinthians 10:12-14).

Thus far in this chapter we have discussed intentional withdrawal. The choice to withdraw may be exercised by letting habits take over or by deciding to avoid situations which are viewed as harmful. But not all withdrawal is conscious. Your body has its own built-in safety mechanisms. When an object approaches your eyes, you automatically flinch. The eyelid closes to protect the eye from harm. Withdrawal may be physical or mental, voluntary or involuntary. It is a way we respond to stress.

DIAGRAM FIVE

WITHDRAWAL

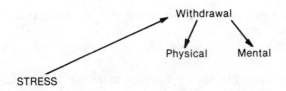

One response to stress is to let go or withdraw from that which is causing the stress. Physical withdrawal implies removing yourself from the source of irritation. Mental withdrawal occurs when the mind blocks out the stress-producing stimulus.

Withdrawal is a protective tool you have to keep you from stress overloads. While withdrawing protects the human system, it does not contribute to growth.

Jane knew she was in trouble when she saw all the downstairs lights on as she approached the driveway. Her parents had specifically instructed her to be in at ten o'clock. After all, it was a school night. And now as the car rolled into the driveway it was after twelve. It was a full ten minutes before the car door finally opened and Jane got out and walked into the house. She realized that her parents were still up and she was pretty sure she knew why.

The only way to get to her bedroom was to go through the living room where they were sitting. Jane tried to appear nonchalant as she entered the room. She greeted her parents with, "Hi, you still up?" It didn't work.

"Sit down, Jane. Your father and I want to talk with you. You were specifically told when you left this evening to be in at ten o'clock . . ."

For the next ten to fifteen minutes, Mother and Father go through a speech they have been rehearsing for the past two hours. Jane doesn't hear a word. She has that magical ability, so often found in teenage children, to switch the dial to off. The words go over her head, not through her ears.

Dad concludes, ". . . so, what do you have to say for yourself, young lady?"

Jane replies, "Oh, okay. I'll do better next time. Can I go to bed now?"

Jane's parents have witnessed mental withdrawal. It is not dissimilar to that all-too-common experience you have in church at times when the pastor is preaching. Nor is it distinctly different from some of those excursions into fantasy that delightfully entice you away from the routine of scheduled activities.

Withdrawal, whether physical or mental, provides no opportunity for growth. It is a way to respond to frustration without increasing the stress. To the extent you are able to shut out the stimuli that have created anxiety, the frustration will not be reinforced.

A husband finds it difficult to talk to his wife when he notices that her eyes are welling and she is going to cry. Every time he reads "the signs" that she is going to be upset and begin to weep, he leaves the house. By leaving his home, the husband removes himself from the source of his stress. A brisk walk works out the kinks and his frustration subsides.

A business executive finds that the well-being of his stomach is directly proportional to the amount of pressure he senses at his desk during an afternoon. He suspects that he may be working himself into an ulcer. One effective way he has found to relieve the tension and pressure is to play a round of golf in the afternoon. He learns that when too many decisions are pressing in on him and he finds himself looking for the bicarb, he can leave those decisions at the office and lose himself in the exhilaration and camaraderie of a good golf game.

Do the decisions and responsibilities melt away while the

executive is out there chipping away with his clubs? At what point does he really need to escape and on what occasions should he develop alternative ways to deal with the pressure?

Is the stress really resolved between the man and his wife when he chooses to kick the dog around the block rather than facing her tears? At what point should the husband take a walk to cool off his anger and frustration and when should he stay by his wife's side and seek to work through their problems?

Conscious action leads to growth. At times it is necessary and wise to withdraw. If we do not withdraw consciously, the body takes over in times of stress in its protective way to do it for us. Don't lose sight of the value of retreating, in letting go, or even in running away when it is warranted.

Remember, though, life is more than a collection of well-worn habits. Living is the opportunity to choose creatively a new challenge, to risk a new path.

Learn to be content, but never be satisfied!

INTERACTION #3

Take time to think back over the past two years. Can you come up with an example of a situation where you gave up too soon? Are there other situations that come to mind where it would have been advantageous to withdraw a little sooner?

Try to develop a list of guidelines, streamlined to fit your situation, that might help you to determine when to persevere and when to back off. For starters, try to come up with three in the first category and three in the second.

4
Responding to Stress: Constructive Action

The little Rambler skims down the two-lane road, unimpeded by traffic, briskly traversing the long straight-away through the Kansas cornfields.

Inside, the man is humming an old Army song while his wife buries her face in the road map.

"Oh!" she says with a little start. "Honey, I've got it figured out. We made a wrong turn back there at Flingley Flats. We're going the wrong way."

The husband keeps on driving and singing.

"Honey—did you hear me? We're headed the wrong direction!"

"Ah, yeah, I know that. But we're making such good time!"

It feels *so good* to make progress toward a goal. The successful completion of any task requires forward motion. Sluggish engines may require warm-up time along the way, but at some point you need to make your decision, slip your ideas into gear, get your foot off the clutch and get rolling.

Carports are great shelters, but the scenery gets a little old after several years. Once you're out of the driveway, momentum begins to build with the rewards of accomplishment throughout the journey.

Sometimes you know where you want to go, but you're not sure of the best route. You've tried good old Highway A and it got you there—eventually. Highway B works too and you have every serpentine swerve committed to memory. But this Highway X looks interesting. It might be a better way. Can you afford the risk of trying a new road? It's a little unnerving. What if it doesn't go where you think it does? What would people say if you ran out of gas or had car trouble? You've got a lot to gain, but then you've got something to lose, too.

Some roads have built-in dangers. Other roads are dead ends. Some roads require great patience and much time for they are difficult routes to travel—shaded rests and vista turnouts are rare to the point of extinction. Each route, however, offers to the traveler the opportunity to learn and make progress. Journeys successfully completed provide a greater number of options when considering which route to take the next time.

You could probably name a half dozen people you know whose selection of roads amounts to a few well-worn ruts. You could plot their course blindfolded because they habitually choose the same track every time. Woe to them if they should ever approach a washed-out bridge or a landslide along the way. "Detour" simply doesn't appear in their vocabulary.

Others you know are flip-side to this sort of thinking. These pathfinders are continually discovering alternate routes and have alerted their senses to seek a better way. Like Robert Frost, they have an incurable tug at the feet to try "the road not taken." They already know the country better than anyone else because the road map is posted on the inside of their eyelids through actual experience. Their willingness to risk and their sensitivity to do what will or won't be productive make the joy of future discoveries inevitable. How many productive roads have you found? Would you be willing to turn your wheels out of the comfortable ruts to try a new track through open country?

Dale and Bonnie have been dating for six months. Dale likes Bonnie. A lot. And that has him worried.

"Hey, maybe this is a little too much," Dale reasons, as he catches himself thinking "serious" thoughts about the young woman. "Maybe we should cool it for a while and think it over. Maybe I should ask her to be friends or something."

Dale is 25. Quiet, studious, at times caught up in the effort to be a perfectionist. Dale doesn't know how to handle the new set of feelings that moves in when he thinks about Bonnie. He's never been down this particular road before and it strikes him as a little risky. Dale lacks confidence to go on and he is asking permission of himself to return to that old comfortable road where he feels safer—less vulnerable.

This new road seems to be lined with every manner of uncertainty. What if he commits himself and Bonnie decides she doesn't care for him? How can he know if he's *really* in love with her? If he genuinely loves Bonnie, why do some of her mannerisms bother him? Are they spending too much time together? What should he do?

Ultimately, Dale will have to answer each of these questions for himself. But the answers won't come until Dale decides that the risk is worthwhile when the goal is worthwhile. The dangerous peaks of growth are better faced than the swamp of stagnation. Is not risk the prerequisite to growth?

Al appeared to have a limitless supply of energy. The civil rights movement had provided a cause into which he could continually pour himself. Not willing to let classes interfere with his education, Al interspersed his studies at college with frequent jaunts to participate in every protest march and civil rights rally within Volkswagen range of the campus. You couldn't help but admire Al's infectious enthusiasm and aggressive spirit. If you were to find someone who knew something of Al's past, however, you might find reason for a deeper amazement.

Six years earlier, a seventeen-year-old Al had huddled in a corner of a world that filled him with fear and insecurity. Al had a drinking problem; he drank as much as he could and as often as he could. He stayed in bed most of the time and seldom left the walls of his studio apartment. What had changed? He met a person, a congressman, who touched his life. This congressman reached into Al's corner and said, "Come out of there. You're worth more than that."

Al believed him and it changed his life. In six years he had become a personable, competent, aggressive young man searching for some answers to the problems of society. Al was willing to give himself to those endeavors he found to be worthwhile. He was growing. Though his life-style produced a certain amount of stress at times, overall it seemed thoroughly worth living.

Stress is inevitable. You live in a world of pressure. You can choose to capitulate, to withdraw, or to take a risk and engage in constructive action. Only the third alternative produces growth.

DIAGRAM SIX

CONSTRUCTIVE ACTION
Leads to Growth

STRESS ━━━━━━━▶ Constructive Action
(The soil for growth)

Stress which encourages you to explore constructive alternatives provides a soil for growth.

Risk is not comfortable, but it is essential if you are to grow.

It isn't possible to take all roads. Select carefully where to invest your energies. Remember, progress against the current takes place one step at a time. Constructive action will provide you with new adaptive behavior which will in turn help to cope with frustration. As you grow, you gain greater versatility to face different stresses. Your few unhappy, rutted roads become a cloverleaf cluster of new options. Not overnight perhaps, but construction is underway.

If your repertoire of responses under stress is limited to

only four alternatives, you have not learned much versatility. If, however, you could choose from fifteen or more alternatives when faced with a stressful situation, you would be a much more creative person. One indicator of the level of maturity in a person might be the number of alternatives perceived when faced with a frustrating problem. The mature person selects, from a full reservoir of alternatives, the most effective response to a given situation.

When you reach the turnoff to a new road, you won't find anyone handing out written guarantees. That's what makes it risky. It is possible, however, to gain information from others before you decide to point your nose in that direction. And if you've had some bad experiences when you dead-ended on a new approach, chances are you won't be brimming with enthusiasm to try that way again.

Don was one of forty boys invited to spend a week hiking and camping in that wild, green world of the Mt. Hood National Forest. Five boys and one adult formed a trail team. The teams traveled several hundred yards apart while on the trail and at night the campsites were staked in close proximity. Fresh-kindled campfires crackled and echoed in the cool darkness, providing a suitable setting for group singing and an inspirational challenge from one of the leaders. It was all so utterly different. Out here in the woods one sensed an aloneness even when he sat with a group around the fire. These young men who would be afraid in most places to let anyone hear them sing could now let go with tremendous gusto.

Later in the night, one or more of the young men could be found sitting around the smaller fires where their trail team had set up camp. There is a special intoxication about the massive firs in the majestic Oregon mountains. Stars you never knew existed fill the sky and seem so close. Allowing yourself to be swallowed by that universe above you is both painful and exquisite. The liquid chatter of the nearby stream reminds you of the consistent way life goes on.

It's an unusual place to think and try to put life together in a meaningful way. Sipping a cup of boiled coffee fresh off the fire, trying to burn some marshmallows or trying not to burn the popcorn—whatever the activity—you feel good. It is a time to reflect and a time to decide what is really important in your life.

During the week, Don and I developed a strong relationship. One night in that small campfire setting, Don related some of the tragic events that had caused him to spend ten months in the state training school. The words came slowly in an old-sounding, detached tone of voice. Don's parents divorced while he was still a baby and numerous occasions of child abuse and neglect had scarred him deeply. When he was fourteen he left home to find his real mother. One night, while drinking with his buddies, he was challenged to steal a car. He accepted the challenge, for as Don said, "No one likes to be called a chicken." Before he was apprehended by the authorities, he had stolen five more cars. By age fifteen he had spent ten months in the state training school for boys.

Friday morning came. Don was up early, and true to his word, was cooking breakfast for me. It was a good day, full of laughter and clowning as well as quiet miles through cathedral forests. But then, the whole week had been good. Rarely had a young person invested so heavily in the camping program as Don had. Surely, I thought, new doors were opening for this troubled young man. That evening Don asked me if we could talk.

Together we walked out across the meadow, around to the other side of the lake. It was a matchless evening in a week of beautiful evenings. A wisp of wind, the clear, wonder-filled sky, and a full moon casting eerie reflections of the mountain onto the lake provided a peaceful and solemn setting for two people to talk.

Don started by expressing appreciation for the week. "This has been the greatest week of my life. I never knew it was possible to have so much fun. I never realized that peo-

ple could care like you and all the others who made this
camping trip possible have cared."

DIAGRAM SEVEN

STRESS CYCLE

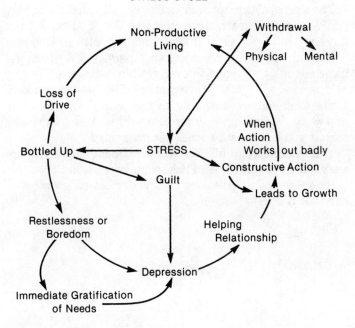

To summarize, stress is responded to in one of three ways:

1. Capitulation, where the irritation is bottled up and eats
    cancerously at the individual;

2. Withdrawal, where the human system is protected from further
    hurt; or

3. Action, where growth begins.

Stress is not good or bad. It is a consequence of living.

51

He went on, "I wanted to tell you this tonight because tomorrow when the bus comes and takes us back to the school, I'm going to forget the whole damn thing."

I was stunned into silence. The week had gone so well. What could have prompted such a negative response? Not knowing what else to say I asked, "Why?"

The memorable response came back from Don. "I'm only fifteen, but I've learned one thing in life. You can't trust anybody but yourself. I'll never put my faith in God and I'll never put my faith in another person. I'll never get close enough to anyone to ever get burned again."

How is it with you? Have you tried and failed so many times that you are unwilling to risk again? Did someone you were depending on let you down, so now you're not sure if you can trust another person again?

There are no guarantees. Disappointment and failure are the regular companions of achievement and fulfillment.

Examine the alternatives. Do you want to grow? You can, but it's risky.

INTERACTION #4

So often as I read through a book or article I find myself asking,"Is this Biblical?" Maybe that's where you are right now. You're asking yourself, "What does the Bible have to say about growth?" Take time to read through the story of David. As you read, make a list of the ten major events in his life. Now try to determine in each event whether David capitulated, withdrew or engaged in meaningful activity. In each case, what was the result?

Try two more case studies. Choose from the lives of Ruth, Peter, Martha, Samson or Paul. From your Biblical investigations what conclusions can you draw about the process of growth?

PART TWO

Footholds Midstream

It's not that we want life to stop—if it would only slow down a little sometimes! Slipping in the stream would not be so bad if the water would wait for a moment while you get back on your feet and regain your balance. But it doesn't work that way. The current crashes on and on and on. Mindless, merciless it seems.

An illness sweeps you off your feet and the process of climbing back to an upright position seems tortuously slow. Life doesn't stop to ask questions; it rushes at you—surges around you, pushing, demanding, heedless of weakness, careless of pain. If the streambed were smooth, there would be little chance of resisting the onrushing flood. The only direction possible would be backwards—head over heels—at the complete mercy and whim of the stream. But there are footholds—firm, immovable resting places to brace against the current and encourage a further step.

From these helpful balance points the up-stream strider may regain a shattered perspective, piece together priorities and catch a glimpse of the way ahead. If you can't stop the water, the next best thing is to learn to progress in spite of it. Or better still, learn how to take charge because of it.

5
An Awareness
of Direction

David Campbell has written a fascinating book entitled, *If You Don't Know Where You're Going, You'll Probably End Up Someplace Else.* Where are you headed in life? What is important to you? What plans have you made to get there?

People change continually. You are a different person than you were last year or five years ago. Why? What happened? What made you change? Were they desired changes, planned changes, or did they happen in spite of yourself? What changes do you expect in your life by this time next year?

It's difficult to produce desired change, isn't it? Undesirable changes seem to occur with alarming ease. It's usually easy to get fat, or become excessively selfish, or to spend ourselves into debt. Downstream changes come readily. It's those upstream changes that require us to take charge of our lives that are so dearly won.

How many times have you decided to lose weight or to start an exercise program or to make new friendships, or whatever, and fallen short of the mark?

Randy's parents set about to effect change in the life of their son. After all, they wanted the best for him. They selected a good college, but Randy's high school grades had been borderline (and often a little south of the border). Unless his academic standing surfaced a few fathoms, the college would not touch him even if he were seven feet tall and played basketball.

In the second quarter of Randy's senior year, he brought home three D's and two C's. Now his parents were really concerned. As an incentive to get Randy to try harder they took away his privilege to drive the car and he was "grounded" until his grades improved. Randy was now highly motivated to change.

Armed with a new and holy zeal he confronted me, his school counselor, with a burning commitment to change.

"Next quarter, I'm going to get straight A's," he announced.

His parents were pleased for they had told Randy many times, "We know you could get straight A's if you would just try."

I watched the next few days with interest. Randy seemed to be trying. Each night he lugged home the books. He reported that he had been studying three or four hours each night. Then the test came. Randy had a theme to write for his English class. After spending hours in writing, editing and polishing his work, Randy turned it in with great pride. Unfortunately, the English teacher was not aware of Randy's hard work or of his commitment to improve his grades. Instead of the usual D, the paper was returned with a high C grade. Randy was discouraged. He didn't make the A for which he had been working. What was the use of trying anyway? The crusader retreated after the first battle in utter defeat, sword tarnished, spirit broken.

What kept Randy from improving his grades? Two points can be observed. The motivation to change came from circumstances which Randy didn't control and didn't like, instead of from within. His desire to change was not based on a need to be accepted by the college, but by his hope to drive the car and to be released from the "grounding" imposed by his parents.

Secondly, Randy set his goals too high. He failed to realize that you don't jump from D's to A's. You move from D's to C's. Most change is gradual.

What change takes place when you become a Christian? It begins with a personal confrontation when one senses his own inadequacy. You realize that God has provided a way to give you new life to replace your inadequate one. As a willful act, you acknowledge your need for God and transformational change takes place in your life. God, on the basis of the redemptive work of His Son, Jesus, accepts you into a new, living relationship with Himself. Guidelines for living are provided through the Bible. You are invited to have conversation with God on a personal, intimate level through prayer. Life has changed.

This process, often referred to as a conversion experience, is not a normal one. God transforms your life through His power and you are changed; you have experienced a miracle. Most change, however, is gradual and continual. It takes place in a sequential way, step by step.

> For I am confident of this very thing, that He who began a good work [transformational change] in you will perfect it [gradual change] until the day of Christ Jesus (Philippians 1:6).

God is not limited and He can change a life dramatically at any time He chooses. People often testify to a struggle they have had for years with a particular problem in their life. Suddenly God delivers them and they are free from that problem. Yet more often, God enables us to grow toward maturity by working through the problem, taking steady steps of progress.

You face struggles in your life. You wrestle with your own secret dilemmas and disappointments. Again and again these personal concerns and anxieties seem to pin you to the mat and keep you from becoming the kind of person you really want to be.

Don't be discouraged by this. Rapid change is difficult to accomplish. When you commit yourself to change at a faster rate than usual, you run the risk of failure. If this is repeated numerous times, you become reluctant to try to change again. As a result, you find yourself in despair with little or no commitment to grow. What is needed is a realistic plan which helps you to take the next step. As you develop this plan and find success in achieving your goal, you are motivated to take the next step—against the current. Growth results.

DIAGRAM EIGHT (A)

HILLS AND VALLEYS

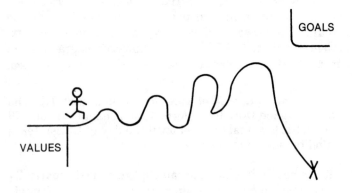

DANGER OF OVER-COMMITMENT

Goals set too high often lead to discouragement or failure. It is better to take one step at a time.

This sort of progress brings much joy, for you are now consciously determining the direction of your life. In taking charge, you begin climbing step by step upstream. Psychologist Carl Rogers has so appropriately stated, "Life is a direction, not a destination."

Perhaps it would be helpful to picture the dynamics of change by imagining a person in a rapidly flowing stream with an ever-changing current. As long as you live change will take place. The current will move you. However, you do not need to just drift. You can choose a direction and start to swim. Some are foolish and swim downstream toward the waterfall. This happens when you engage in self-destructive behavior. Others see a distant point of glorious fulfillment and slowly, one stroke at a time, head upstream in that direction. It would be nice if we were able to pull ourselves out of the water and fly upstream closer to the desired destination, then drop back in again, but that is not possible. The stream is life and in the stream we stay. Strength comes as we work our way upstream. We learn to swim better through swimming. It can be done. Others have gone before. It is worth the struggle.

Therefore, since we have so great a cloud of witnesses surrounding us, let us also lay aside every encumbrance, and the sin which so easily entangles us, and let us run with endurance the race that is set before us (Hebrews 12:1-2).

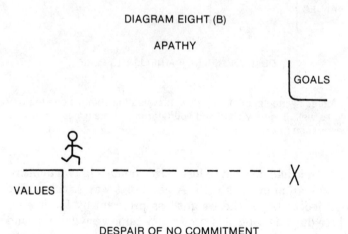

DIAGRAM EIGHT (B)

APATHY

GOALS

VALUES

DESPAIR OF NO COMMITMENT

If you've tried and failed numerous times, it may be hard to get up and try again. But it's worth the effort.

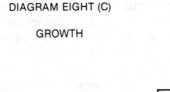

DIAGRAM EIGHT (C)

GROWTH

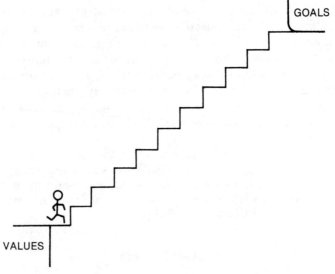

DEVELOPMENT OF A REALISTIC PLAN

A step-by-step plan of growth with evaluation points along the way works well. Begin by clarifying your starting points (values) and your destination (goals).

Joanne had decided to lose thirty pounds in two months. It was an ambitious plan. A good diet was selected. She decided to begin the weight-loss program by fasting for three days. During this time she became very irritable and found she was unable to sleep. When she started on the diet she had frequent headaches. Finally, discouraged, Joanne abandoned the diet and went on a two-day binge, gorging herself with food. The net result was that she gained five pounds instead of losing thirty. Such frustration could have been avoided if Joanne had evaluated her diet and made adjustments in the first few days. Evaluation and adjustment do not imply defeat. In fact, they may prove to be the better part of victory.

Early in the Civil War, Union General Burnside was determined to gain a certain piece of ground by a direct frontal assault on a certain long, low stone fence. Believing his plan to be the only logical method of advance, the General sent wave after wave of young Union soldiers into the withering blaze of confederate musket and cannon fire coming from behind the wall. Attack after attack sent hundreds—thousands—of boys and men to their death; still the General persisted. It was only after the better part of his army lay dead or dying some several hundred feet short of the objective that Burnside became willing to consider an alternate plan.

How much better it would have been to take the first small loss, dreadful as it was, and make a new battle plan rather than to sacrifice gallons of Yankee blood on the altar of his unyielding stubbornness. The battle of Fredricksburg might have been a Union victory instead of a heartrending defeat.

Real, identifiable change for the better requires time. A farmer, wishing to help a troubled young man, made arrangements with the state school for boys to have Rick live in his home. The farm would be a good place for Rick to learn to work with his hands, and he would have the encouragement of the farmer working side by side with him. For a time, things went very well. The home provided warmth and love Rick had never known. He sensed that here were people who really cared for him. But after five months in the farmer's home, Rick ran away.

The authorities apprehended him and brought him back. With a forgiving heart, the farmer agreed to try again if Rick wanted to come back. One month later Rick ran away again. This time when he was brought back, the farmer said, "Return him to the state school. He doesn't appreciate what my wife and I are trying to do for him."

With some wisdom, the parole officer replied, "Rick spent seventeen years becoming what he is now. You can't hope to change him in six months."

Change is gradual. For a time, progress may simply mean that you stop swimming downstream. You may not yet be ready to move upstream, but at least you have stopped doing things that are self-destructive. Patience is required, for many of us, like Rick, spent a long time getting where we are and it's a long way back.

How about taking that first step? More will be said later on how to build a plan, but right now you need to evaluate where you are going. No one becomes an alcoholic overnight. One drink leads to another, which leads to yet another and another, until finally a person finds himself trapped. One doesn't become a philosopher overnight either. Rather, one bit of wisdom built upon another erects the thoughtful counsel of a sage.

Consider the athlete. Hours of training, mental concentration, strenuous exercise and proper rest and diet form a lifestyle. After many competitive events—many false starts and scratches—the day arrives when he or she wins the first race. He doesn't start by attaining the Olympic gold medal. He works to win the first race.

Perhaps you have known defeat for more years than you would care to divulge. It doesn't matter. You can be a winner and you can start now by taking the first step. It begins by taking stock of where you are right now—assessing your present condition. But don't dwell on that. The stream lies ahead. The next step begins where every statesman, scholar or Olympic champion must begin—against the current. In the right direction.

INTERACTION #5

List the most significant change in each of the following areas within the time limits indicated.

	In the last 30 days	In the last year	In the last 5 years
SOCIAL			
FAMILY			
SPIRITUAL			
OCCUPATIONAL			
PERSONAL			

Now go back and put a star by any of those changes which you consciously made happen. Can you think of one commitment to change in each area that has failed? In a sentence or two, what do you feel has been the principal reason for your failure in each category?

6
Faith, The Firm Footing

You may have heard the story before. The wheelbarrow brimmed with bricks. Flexing his hands once or twice and drawing his lungs full of fresh autumn air, a lone man pushed the load ahead of him on a two-and-quarter-inch tightrope over Niagara Falls. The assembled hordes gaped and gasped as the brick-pusher calmly directed his load above the great spill of thunder below. Death awaited his first misstep.

But no! He arrived on the other side without jostling a single brick and the crowds dissolved into ecstatic applause for such a balanced individual.

At this, the daredevil selected a young man from the crowd and inquired in a voice that boomed over the falls, "Do you believe I can walk across those falls on that rope, pushing a wheelbarrow in front of me?"

"Well yeah, sure I do," the young man affirmed. "I believe you can do it. I just saw you do it."

"Very well, my boy, if you really believe, climb into my wheelbarrow and I'll take you back across the rope with me."

The young man remembered a previous engagement and melted rather suddenly into the audience. The challenge was too great for his faith.

Faith is trust in the ability of someone or something that enables us to take constructive action based on that trust. You might describe faith as trust in motion. In a small way, you exercise faith every time you sit in a chair.

"That doesn't sound very theological," you say. Perhaps not, but it is certainly an example of trust in motion. Every time you walk into a room and are offered a seat by your smiling host, you exercise confidence that the chair is capable of holding you up.

Or maybe you're the type who likes to test the chair a little to see if it might be wobbly. If it flunks the test, you smile back at your host and sit in another chair, worthier of your trust. By such a meticulous process, you might save yourself the embarrassment of collapsing someone's furniture, right?

On the other hand, people might think it strange to see you wandering about the room, turning chairs and couches over to examine their structural reliability. It looks a little weird. Certainly you would come under suspicion if this sort of ceremony was observed each time you visited in a particular home. How many visits would it take before someone would stop you in the midst of your examination and say, "It's okay. You can sit in that chair. Really, you don't need to overhaul it today. It's held up people much heavier than you."

You learn on the basis of previous experience which chairs to sit in and which chairs to avoid. Examination isn't really necessary unless you've had advance word of a termite convention in the immediate vicinity.

Faith could be considered in three dimensions: faith in things, faith in people, and faith in God. In each of these dimensions, faith requires a focal point somewhere beyond your own resources. Faith is something known inside that demands an outward expression. After all the examining and evaluating, you take a step. You do something. You act on the basis of what you know and how you feel. Your thinking and your feeling may not always agree, but both need to be considered before you act.

In what *things* should you place your faith? We all trust in "things." The real question is whether a particular material object will increase or decrease your level of productivity. Faith in that good old horseless chariot to get you to work will give you greater time on the job than if you had to walk five miles each way. But faith in those little blue pills to get you to sleep at night may make you groggy and counterproductive the next day.

We live in a world of things and only a fool would deny his daily dependence on them. But what level of faith should be placed in things? Men have poured their lives into an estate only to see it obliterated by a quick stroke of an auditor's ball-point pen. Build your house of a thousand dreams and a fire may gut it all in a thousand seconds. Invest every spare buck and every waking minute in molding your antique Pierce-Arrow and some drunk in a '58 Volkswagen could run a red light and broadside you.

Is it possible to enjoy those things which enhance life, to place faith in them and use them in a beneficial way without making them our master? Is it possible to let things serve us without allowing that relationship to be reversed? It's painful to lose something in which we've heavily invested. Yet that very pain reminds us that our principal shareholdings should appear on heaven's "big board." Our investments are to be eternal investments.

> . . . "Beware, and be on your guard against every form of greed; for not even when one has an abundance does his life consist of his possessions."
>
> And he told them a parable, saying, "The land of a certain rich man was very productive. And he began reasoning to himself, saying, 'What shall I do, since I have no place to store my crops?' And he said, 'This is what I will do: I will tear down my barns and build larger ones, and there I will store all my grain and my goods. And I will say to my soul, "Soul, you have many goods laid up for many years to come; take your ease, eat, drink and be merry." '
>
> "But God said to him, 'You fool! This very night your soul is required of you; and now who will own what you have prepared?' So is the man who lays up treasure for himself, and is not rich toward God" (Luke 12:15-21).

Faith in people starts with faith in yourself. When the reservoir of self-esteem is full and overflowing you are enabled to trust and to help others, receiving the same confidence and aid from them.

Faith is confidence in the ability of another person which enables us to take constructive action. Rev up your imagination for a moment and picture yourself perched precariously on a narrow ledge. You've just stumbled from the trail above and landed fortuitously on a little outcropping of the sheer cliff. If you weren't so scared, you'd be embarrassed. Your point of departure was some twenty feet above—straight up. A canyon yawns several hundred feet below you—straight down. There you are—stranded in your stratospheric position with only a good set of lungs to elicit support. Perhaps another hiker from the trail will hear your anguish and come to your rescue.

You are much relieved when you see a rope slide tantalizingly before your face from somewhere above. A voice says, "Grab ahold, honey. Dear, dear, let's see if we can get you back on this nice trail."

A pleasant prospect . . . but that voice . . . you glance skyward to see who is holding the rope.

At first glance your spirit leaps with the thrill of recognition, "Gramma!"

You can't help but smile as you look up at the smiling face of that sweet old lady. "Man, does she ever bake a mouth-massaging batch of molasses cookies. Knits a great shawl, too. And she looks so cute up there with that big rope in her bony little hands . . ."

Then it hits you. "My stars, the rope. Why, she couldn't weigh over ninety pounds wringing wet. If there were ten of her, she couldn't pull me off this ledge."

You thank her for her offer to help, smile, and wave her on her way. To grab hold of the rope would mean plunging both of you down the canyon.

Was there a lack of trust in your grandmother? No, not at all. Your grandmother would do everything in her power to help you, gladly risking her life. The reticence to take hold of the rope was not due to lack of trust. It wasn't her reliability you questioned; it was her ability. Both ingredients are necessary in a faith relationship—confidence and competence.

Ability by itself isn't enough either. Picture the same setting. You're sitting dejectedly on that same ledge, watching two or three hawks circle among the clouds below you (or are they vultures?). Down swings the rope again, only this time there is a huge hunk of manflesh at the other end. The guy looks big enough to play left tackle for the Chicago Bears. (Is that where you've seen him? That face . . .)

There is little question as to this rescuer's ability. He could pull you up and down all day like a yo-yo. Ah! Then it hits you. That's the yo-yo you sold your car to only two weeks ago. You've had a few heated conversations on the phone with him since then. He's accused you of prior knowledge in regards to that cracked engine block, and he's been rather forceful in pressing the point. Do you detect a slight smirk on his face as he shouts down, "Grab ahold!"

Again, you politely decline. After all, the view is terrific. This time your reluctance has nothing to do with the person's ability. No problem there. It's just that you don't trust the man. He might let the rope slip through his fingers when you get halfway to the top and all you would have to remember as you sky-dived to your doom would be his final remark, "Oops."

When you place your faith in another person, you expect good things to happen. That person has certain resources or abilities which are made available to you. The combination of resources from within you and from within the other person blend together to give you the confidence needed to do what needs to be done. Faith grows as you have opportunity to know others better. A climate of openness and trust brings out the potential abilities which are available to you as you learn about your friends. These people serve as resource banks from whom you can draw that which is needed in order to grow through your activities.

You have heard people say, "Whenever I need help, I go to my friend. He or she always seems to have the right word for my situation." This is a statement of faith. It is well-founded faith when based on a pre-established record of deserved trust and true competence.

Faith in God is confidence in the competence of God that enables us to do those things which would please Him. It is "the assurance of things hoped for, the conviction of things not seen . . ." (Hebrews 11:1).

God invites you to know Him better so you can trust Him more. As you respond to this beautiful, open invitation you begin to grow in faith. You can risk more for God because you know that He is completely reliable. He is competent and He will do exactly as He says. He has extended the rope to you in love and He is fully able to handle His end of the arrangement.

If your belief does not result in action, it is not faith. It is merely acceptance or acknowledgment of a truth without the willingness to invest in that knowledge. Faith takes hold of the rope and steps off the ledge into open air. Faith is the willingness to get into the wheelbarrow and let the tightrope walker take you over the falls. When you have faith in something or someone, the result is action. It will be reflected in what you do. (See Hebrews 11:4-10.)

Faith is a solid, firm footing which gives assurance in an insecure, changing world where footholds are hard to find. Too often people think of faith as some ethereal, mystical unknowable sort of operation. Faith is not stepping blindfolded off a cliff hoping to find a pillow to catch you at the bottom.

A soldier is given orders to seek out and disarm a number of land mines beneath a harmless-looking field of crabgrass. In preparing himself for the task, the soldier dutifully blindfolds his eyes, puts plugs in his ears, then gropes his way forward, stomping here and there to locate his first mine. Obviously, the first one will be his last one.

There'll be no time to yell, "Sarge, I found it." As soon as he detects the first land mine it will be time to call for another volunteer.

"Well, that's stupid," you say. Yes it is! But it's an accurate picture of the way some people view faith. Checking their brains out to lunch, they launch out on a plan that is doomed from the beginning. It looks a whole lot more like foolishness than faith.

God has given to you great resources—yours and His—to be used wisely. Don't hold back. Growth requires challenging the current and making upstream mileage. Life comes fast and hard sometimes. It's wise to be well-equipped, wise to make a careful choice of routes and wise to remember that headway happens one step at a time.

INTERACTION #6

If someone were to ask you to name five things on which you rely heavily, what would they be? List them on a piece of paper. But don't stop there. Force yourself to assign priority to these five things, starting with the most important and working your way down to the least important.

Now write down the five most important people in your life. Can you put your finger on one specific personal gain that each of these relationships has brought your way?

Now it gets stickier. List five other people to whom *you* have contributed significantly. Can you do it? Again, be specific as to what each contribution was.

Finally, search your own heart and record five things which your faith in God enables you to do.

7
Time and the Level of Importance

Sunday morning teased at the windows like a family cat that wanted everyone to wake up and let him in.

Cautious glances at the sky following the morning church service confirmed the miracle to everyone's satisfaction. The sun was shining in Oregon and it was going to be a no-holds-barred kind of day for a picnic. Several cars made short work of the Tualatin River Highway and pulled into good old Louie's picnic ground all at once, like a highway patrol in an old movie.

After lunch a cluster of the kids went down to a wooden dock overhanging the river to lean on the rail and watch the water.

One little boy knew better than to lean over the railing. But the other kids were watching—really watching—so he had to demonstrate the limits of his bravado. Logs waiting for the mill had been corralled in the river below. Few of the parents were even watching when this little boy, with a short cry, suddenly plummeted over the edge. Almost miraculously he did not hit any of the logs. Yet—I was only seven years old and I had not learned how to swim.

Fortunately, an older brother had been keeping an eye on my attention-hungry antics. Ripping off his shirt, kicking the shoes from his feet, Dave hurled himself into the water after me. Dave's activities gained the attention of other members of the family and friends, and they surged onto the wooden dock and leaned over the railing to watch the rescue effort.

It may have been only a few minutes. It seemed longer—much longer. The water was still where the boys had gone in. Then all heads jerked to a point of erupting water fifty or sixty feet down river where Dave suddenly emerged with me in tow. Swimming quickly to the shore, Dave helped pull his little brother out of the water before he himself collapsed on the dock. Knowledgeable hands applied artificial respiration and my life was spared.

Later that afternoon as the family gathered their belongings to head for home, God and Dave received some heartfelt praise. It was chilling to think how close . . . but it was a time to be thankful.

Some decisions must be made very quickly. If you see a toddler pumping his new-found legs toward a busy street, there is little time to contemplate what to do. You take action. Right away. You yell or you run after the child to save him from the impending danger. If you waited to consider what the best alternative might be, if you "took five" to weigh all your options, the child could die. The situation screams for immediate, reflexive movement—action!

Other decisions can be set aside until a later time without seriously altering the consequences of the decision. How many of us have postponed a decision to paint the house? "Ah, the paint'll last another winter. I'll get around to it next year," you tell yourself. The wild moss green you purchased for that irresistible discount at the paint shop last February gathers another layer of dust around its unpried lid. The Oakland Raiders win another one.

It's true, hasty decisions may lead you into situations that you later regret. On the other hand, putting off decisions that need to be made can overload your transformer as the current of guilt and frustration builds up—behind your do-it-later switch. Knowing when to decide, when to take action, helps to keep the day-to-day process of living in a healthy polarity.

Not only is timing essential, but a proper perspective of how important a decision will be is necessary. Many decisions will dramatically alter your future and need to be given careful consideration. Other decisions are so trivial that it really doesn't matter what you decide in terms of the future consequences. Those decisions should not be as difficult to handle. The decision to choose a marriage partner is more important than whether you should wear your green socks, or your checkered socks, or any socks at all, for that matter. Vocational choice requires weightier deliberation than whether to have pie, ice cream, or both for dessert.

DIAGRAM NINE

MAKING DECISIONS

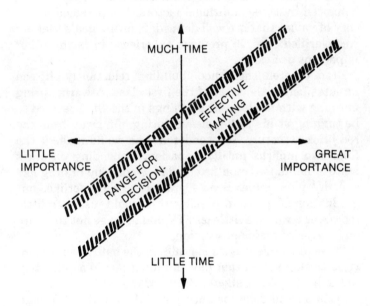

It is hard to make important decisions when you have to do so quickly. More time is needed to gain additional information so you can choose wisely.

Minor decisions should be made and acted upon without delay. This frees you to give attention to those matters of greater consequence.

Decisions made prior to careful consideration of the consequences may result in "prisons of your own making." Decisions delayed which are relatively insignificant may complicate and clutter up your life to the extent you find little time to think through more important questions.

Ideally, the level of importance should be proportional to the amount of time required to make the decision. Did you catch that? Let's breeze it by one more time. If your decision is extremely important, you need a longer time to work on it. If it's a little less vital, you need a little less time. And so it goes.

The ability to make important decisions wisely will be enhanced by three additional factors: 1) a personal inventory of values that are well-defined; 2) future goals that are well-clarified; and, 3) previous experience in facing other important decisions.

Brad entered the school building reluctantly, fifteen minutes before the start of the first class. A warm spring morning with fresh far-away things in the wind seemed to be tugging at his jacket sleeve, luring him away from the red brick structure. He wondered if he would make it the final two months until graduation. Depending on one's state of mind, two months could race-horse by or drag like a balky plow mule. Brad's grades were borderline, but graduation still looked possible if he could just do a little more work, watch a little less TV and manage not to create any waves of major proportion.

Three of Brad's friends met him in the hall. Brad was invited to skip school that day and join them in a quick trip to the beach. What should Brad do?

Certain results can be anticipated if Brad decides to go with his friends. He will miss a major examination in mathematics which cannot be made up. The school will check his absence, and his parents will be notified that he willfully chose not to attend classes. Chances are good the school will suspend him for one to three days if they find out he has skipped.

Weighing this sort of input, it doesn't appear that throwing aside classes to accept the invitation of his friends would be a very wise decision for Brad. What does he decide to do? He goes to the beach. It was an important decision for Brad. He jeopardized graduation from high school to spend a day with three not-so-close friends at the beach.

When Brad returned from the ocean that evening, he realized that he would be in trouble with his parents. He and his buddies had stayed later than they should have. There was no way to cover up. He would have to tell Mom and Dad that he had not gone to school. But Brad was having too good a time to talk to his parents right then. He decided to go see his girlfriend, Judy, instead of going home.

Judy and Brad had been dating for three months. She liked him a lot, but it bothered her that they parked so much. Every evening they spent together, Brad pushed her a little bit more to do things that she had been told were wrong. That evening Brad asked Judy to go for a ride with him in his car. Judy accepted. They drove around until they came to a special parking place Brad had selected up a back road. Brad had decided. Tonight he and Judy were going to "make it." After they had necked for a while, Brad asked his girlfriend to prove her love for him by "going all the way." Judy had never faced this decision before. What should she do? She wanted to please Brad, but she wasn't sure it was right.

It was late when Brad finally arrived home. The lights were out. He wouldn't have to explain to his folks about skipping school until morning. He felt badly about Judy and quite guilty. She had finally given in. He had "scored."

Brad and Judy continued dating about six months before Judy got pregnant. She had made an important decision that night in Brad's car. It changed her life. After the baby was born, Judy continued to live with her folks.

Mom took care of the baby during the day while Judy worked.

Brad was gone. He had argued a great deal with his folks, failed two courses spring semester and didn't graduate. When work got boring, he and a friend decided to take off and travel. No one was sure where they had gone.

Brad and Judy carry irreversible scars from making momentous life decisions without carefully thinking through the consequences of their actions. They decided too quickly on choices that were extremely important. Neither Brad nor Judy had developed an adequate inventory of personal values. Future goals had not been well-clarified, so each lives with the consequences. Each will never be the same. Isn't it ironic that we are responsible for our decisions and must live with the inevitable results even when we act irresponsibly?

The Bible tells us that Isaac and Rebekah had twin sons. The older one they named Esau; the younger, Jacob:

> When the boys grew up, Esau became a skillful hunter, a man of the field; but Jacob was a peaceful man, living in tents. Now Isaac loved Esau, because he had a taste for game; but Rebekah loved Jacob.

> And when Jacob had cooked stew, Esau came in from the field and he was famished; and Esau said to Jacob, "Please let me have a swallow of that red stuff there, for I am famished." Therefore his name was called Edom. But Jacob said, "First sell me your birthright."

> And Esau said, "Behold, I am about to die; so of what use then is the birthright to me?" And Jacob said, "First swear to me"; so he swore to him, and sold his birthright to Jacob. Then Jacob gave Esau bread and lentil stew; and he ate and drank, and rose and went on his way. Thus Esau despised his birthright" (Genesis 25:27-34).

Values don't appear like a fairy-godmother to warn those in the passion of an emotional moment. If they haven't appeared before then, odds lean heavily that they won't, no matter how vital the decision.

When Esau learned later the magnitude of the gift he had pawned away for a plate of stew, he wailed like a widow bereaved. But it was too late. The deal was sealed. The food was only a flickering memory and the inheritance was buttoned in his brother's hip pocket.

When the crucial moment had arrived, Esau's nose and belly and drooling tongue had decided the fate of his birthright. The red stuff smelled good. Esau wanted to warm the underside of his camel-hair leisure suit. There was no debate, no opposing value structure to question his animal response. It felt good and he did it.

Values aren't developed in the trembling moment of crisis. They are forged in the intrapersonal struggles of everyday living and sharpened in the interpersonal communications of meaningful relationships.

"Iron sharpens iron, So one man sharpens another" (Proverbs 27:17).

Have you ever been approached with that ridiculous question, "Do you walk to work or carry your lunch?"

The humor of the question lies in the fact that the two parts are totally unrelated. The inquirer is not really interested in either part of the question. He's trying to be funny.

What would you think of a person who took the question seriously? All day he mulled its ramifications. At home that evening he told his mate, "Honey, I've been challenged today. Do you think I should walk to work or carry my lunch?" The person then continues to expound advantages and disadvantages of walking to work as against the advantages and disadvantages of carrying a lunch.

Wouldn't you tend to think that this person was giving the question a little more attention than it deserved? Really, it was never meant to be taken seriously in the first place. Would you not expect the person to chuckle, throw a quick punch at the inquirer's shoulder and let the question drop from his thinking?

It is possible to carry around questions which are relatively unimportant and could be resolved quickly if you decided to resolve them. Once those questions have been answered, you are free to deal with the more important issues. When you fail to answer a minor question, you begin to use up a great deal of energy that could be better expended. Besides that, it goes over with your friends like sand in the potato salad.

Have you ever been in a restaurant when a friend can't decide what to order? Everyone else at the table has placed his order and sketched a couple of landscapes on the dinner napkins. The waitress is standing there tapping a pencil on the order pad and chewing her gum a little too quickly. The longer the person deliberates, the more uncomfortable you become.

"Let's see . . . how much is the souffle? Oh, there it is, heh-heh . . . right on the menu, yes sir. Now there's the omelet, but I've already had my three eggs this week. Ohhh . . . uh . . . how about . . . no . . . I really don't feel like chowder. Besides, it's Tuesday, wellll . . ."

As the blood pressure of everyone around the table mounts, you may even speak up and offer a suggestion or two.

"Hey, have you tried their chef salad? Doesn't that sound good? Wait'll you taste their roquefort!"

If your friend pulls this stuttering act repeatedly when you go out to eat, it may become a source of irritation that detracts from your relationship.

You think, "I don't understand why this person can't make up his mind about what to eat. It ruins my whole lunch." You choose to find another friend with whom to dine.

Effective decision-making properly balances the amount of time with the level of importance. *Important* questions are weighed carefully. Time is taken to examine the consequences of each alternative.

After the matter is chewed and re-chewed, an appropriate moment arrives for swallowing and stepping out with the decision. It should not be left unresolved for too long, for failure to decide ultimately becomes its own decision.

It is like trying to decide whether to go to the ball game and not making up your mind to go until the ball game is over. You might as well have packed away your pennant and enjoyed an hour playing with your kids.

Less important questions which can be resolved quickly should be decided and dropped from your thinking. Don't rush and don't stall. Set a steady pace as you find those all-important footholds upstream.

INTERACTION #7

We face decisions every day. Little ones and not-so-little ones. After a few minutes of realistic recollection, list ten decisions that you will face within the next year.

1.

2.

3.

4.

5.

6.

7.

8.

9.

10.

Having numbered these decisions, place the number in the spot on the chart below which best describes the time needed to make the decision and the relative level of importance of the decision.

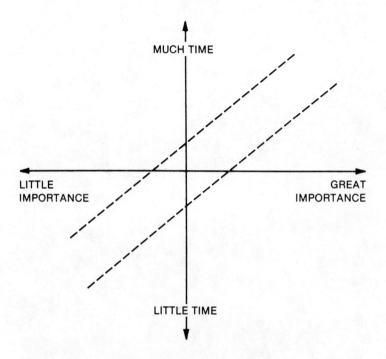

Do you have them placed? On the basis of your chart, then, make three of the decisions right now. Set a time limit not to exceed 30 days on four others. Concerning your remaining three decisions, set up an advantage/disadvantage sheet for each one. Add to this sheet regularly as considerations come to your mind.

8
Treading Water

After four hundred years, slavery must have fit the Israelites like an old shoe. It was one thing to talk about kicking it off and slipping on something new but it was another thing to actually step barefoot into the Sinai and a new way of life.

Even as little as they'd tasted of it, the former slaves were enjoying this thing called "freedom." No chains, no cracking whip—just walking through the desert to a "promised land" that "flowed with milk and honey." Not a bad prospect! Let's hear it for *freedom*!

Meanwhile, back in Egypt, Pharaoh was letting his breakfast get cold as he scowled out the window at the desert. Why had he let those slaves slip out the back door? Who did they think they were, removing their bodies from his Imperial Service? Not only that, they had waltzed away with half the gold in Egypt at the same time.

It wasn't long before Pharaoh was sounding "general quarters." Then, with his top cavalry troop rolling behind him, he set off in a cloud to snap the cuffs on his "escaped slaves."

When the people of Israel saw the Egyptians coming after them, they were frightened:

Then they said to Moses, "Is it because there were no graves in Egypt that you have taken us away to die in the wilderness? Why have you dealt with us in this way, bringing us out of Egypt? Is this not the word that we spoke to you in Egypt, saying, 'Leave us alone that we may serve the Egyptians'? For it would have been better for us to serve the Egyptians than to die in the wilderness" (Exodus 14:11-12).

What would you do if you were in that situation? Would

you surrender your freedom and return to being treated like an animal in Egypt?

Remember, the Israelites had just walked out of a sand-trap and were now nose-to-nose with a water hazard, the Red Sea. No one was ready to punch it out with Pharaoh's hard guys. Would it end like this? With a taste—just an illusory taste—of freedom?

Israel could have set an Olympic speed record for forgetting. They forgot that it was God who had booked them for a one-way flight out of Egypt and it was God who would meet every problem encountered along the way. He hadn't brought them out into the desert to get shot up by Pharaoh's heavies. He would lead them, provide for them and deliver them from threatening situations. And He would bring them to the land He had promised. God wanted His people to trust in Him, to exercise faith and to stop doubting.

Perhaps you are one who feels that questioning and doubting are actually two names for the same highway. It isn't so. Questioning and doubting involve two very different approaches to situations in life.

Questioning, to begin with, is as healthy as a good sneeze. It is a process that provides you with the input or data necessary to determine the best direction in making a choice. Through questioning, you examine the alternatives and set out on the path which will lead to desired results. Questioning has no reluctance. Its gears grind out forward motion. With its feet shod in confidence, questioning grips the banner and risks whatever waits around the corner. It characterizes a life of faith.

Doubting is rooted in debilitating fear. It is the antithesis of faith. Doubting says, "Be careful. You don't have enough information yet. Hold back." It is an excuse for treading water rather than moving ahead. A baseball player who refuses to pick up the bat will never strike out, but then again, he'll never get to first base either. Conscious growth is only possible when there is a personal commitment to risk fighting the current, to progress one step upstream.

Growing is not necessarily comfortable. You're stepping out of the nice warm dugout into the glare, noise and tension of the batter's box. You often wonder with the Israelites of old, "What am I doing out here in this wilderness? I should have stayed back in that ol' slave shack in Egypt. The carpet may have been worn and the roof leaked like the Nile, but at least I was safe."

There are times when you feel certain you hear the sound of a chain saw right after you've crawled out on a long limb. At other times, your decision may make you feel abandoned and alone. Was it wise to have taken the step, to risk growing? If your adventure succeeds, the answer will surge back strongly, "Yes! It was wise." If you fail, it will be necessary to pick up the pieces, learn from your experience and find another road on which to begin again.

Lois seems to have an unending supply of energy. Like a perpetual motion machine, she cranks out nonstop doing, doing, doing. It is a rare occasion when you see her sit down to rest for even a minute. Does that make you think of anyone? Perhaps there is a similar person of your own acquaintance whom you've watched with wide-eyed admiration. Before you commend this person too highly, look carefully. That ceaseless movement might represent a deliberate detour around decision-making. It might be an excuse to tread water.

"Now, wait a minute," you protest. "No one works harder than Lois. She's the spark plug on seventeen different committees. Everyone thinks she's incredible. I don't know anyone who accomplishes more than she does."

Yes, Lois is busy, but is she growing? It's possible to program your life so heavily that you don't have to decide anything. Worthwhile activities fill your schedule from early in the morning until bedtime at night. While you may appear to be productive, you are not consciously growing. Instead, you are "cranking out" life without accepting personal responsibility for what you do. This is a most subtle way to run from pressing decisions and who dares to criticize? You've been too busy tending to demanding duties to look out for yourself.

In a little booklet entitled, *The Tyranny of the Urgent,* the author points out how easy it is to surrender important decisions in order to take care of urgent concerns. Take inventory. Has your life become so full of urgent duties that you never get around to those important personal decisions?

The plumbing is leaky. Household accounts need balancing. Junior needs coaching in his algebra. Then there are those storm windows. Who has time to sit down and analyze where life is taking you? Who has time to pray with the wife or husband over future ministry possibilities? The freight train is rolling too fast to stop and check the map. It's hang on for dear life.

Another cop-out to moving ahead is that old nemesis, procrastination. It's so easy to put off something that you have wanted to do. Let's say that you've wanted to start reading the Bible regularly. You decide that you should set a schedule so time will be available for Bible reading. Until you take the initial step to make a schedule and determine when to begin, it won't happen.

How would you start a plan to begin reading the Bible? Would you commit yourself to a half hour a day for seven days a week? No! That's like trying to jump from D's to A's without recognizing that we move from D's to C's.

Start with a trial plan. Pick an acceptable time and schedule ten minutes for reading on two evenings next week. Determine beforehand where you want to read. After you finish reading, set aside an additional twenty minutes to discuss what you've read with your mate or a personal friend. At the end of two weeks, evaluate your program and make adjustments. Perhaps you will want to add five minutes for a prayer, increase the reading time from ten to fifteen minutes, or from two to three days a week.

The hardest thing to do sometimes is to get started. You want to and you know you should, but something or someone causes you to put the decision off. Dip your toe into the stream. It's cold and the current is fast, but you've committed yourself. It's a beginning.

If you were to ask people what they wanted most in life, the answer from many would come back in one form or another, "I want to be happy." Recipes for happiness, though urgently sought, are rarely found. The famous psychiatrist, Viktor Frankl, says happiness does not come from direct pursuit. Happiness is a by-product when you find meaning in your life. When people fail to find meaning in their lives, the sense of inner emptiness erodes into desperation. They seek any number of substitute experiences. Some grapple for power. Others rush into a funhouse maze of pleasurable activities. Still others try to induce "chemical happiness" through alcohol or drugs.

Research has been done with rats whereby the sensation of eating a meal or having an orgasm was generated by stimulating a part of the rat's brain. When rats were placed on high frequency schedules over a period of several weeks, it was discovered that the rodents would not return to normal functions of eating or sex. They had replaced the simulated experience for the real thing.

While research is limited, there is some indication that a similar response may be generated in the heavy alcohol or drug user. Frequent and heavy stimulation by chemicals, whether in the form of alcohol or drugs, may generate a crippling apathy in a user's life. The person becomes content to sit in a rocking chair while the rest of the world goes by. Dependency and satisfaction produced through this chemically-induced happiness may be sufficient to make the participant reluctant to return to the "real" world. A world of make-believe becomes the greatest of all excuses for treading water. In this sort of world, you see life only as you want it to be, not as it really is.

Dean didn't have any plans when he graduated from

high school. Since jobs weren't that plentiful, he decided to enlist in the United States Navy. That lasted nineteen months. The Navy was persuaded that Dean was using drugs and gave him an uncontested general discharge.

Still unsure as to what he wanted to do, Dean moved into the city to live with some friends. It was difficult to get work and even harder to hang on to a job once Dean had found one. Discouraged by his inability to maintain steady employment, Dean decided to settle for the unemployment checks which resulted from his time in the Navy.

Life was monotonously the same. Dean would get up around noon, smoke a joint or two, eat a little food if it was available, and spend the afternoon tinkering. In late afternoon or early evening, friends would come by and a party would start. The party would last until people had left or "crashed." About noon the next day, the process would begin all over again, and so it went day after day.

At this time, I was counseling at a community college. I got a call from Dean who wanted to come to see me. He was tired of "bumming around" and wanted to get some training for a job. Besides, his unemployment compensation was about to run out.

We set up an appointment for the next week, but Dean didn't show. Four weeks later he called me again, requesting an appointment. "Okay Dean, but what happened last time?"

"Oh, I didn't need to see you, Dr. McMinn. I got an extension on my unemployment."

The drugs that Dean had been using, at first to help him face the real world, had become a world in themselves. He was content to live in a drug world letting society support him rather than to face the responsibilities of providing for himself.

Dean's story would be sad if it ended there, but it didn't. Loving parents prayed for their son. Dean began to get a new perspective. He realized the futility of the life he had been living. His "friends" were not really friends at all. He decided to move home. This time Dean had a different view of his parents. Values imparted in earlier years through the home and through the church became important. Dean started going to church again. People were friendly. The pastor was easy to talk to.

It's been more than three years since Dean became a Christian. During that time, he has worked through an apprenticeship and become a skilled craftsman. He no longer lives at home because he has married and obtained a home of his own.

Not all the problems are solved. Although there are still times when Dean slips back into those self-destructive behaviors, he has become a productive, growing person. Dean got tired of treading water. Pushing out into the main current, he has accepted responsibility for what he will become.

Have you?

INTERACTION #8

Perhaps, in some small degree, you can identify with Dean. Perhaps there are a number of areas in your life where you've settled for the status quo. And things are getting stagnant. So now you are trying to decide if you can really get something moving again.

It is at this point you need to exercise caution. Move too fast and you'll be back at ground zero in record time counting your bruises. Don't try to leap the mountain; *climb* it.

Make a list of ten different actions you would like to consider in the next 30 days. Write each one on a separate piece of paper. Now, arrange the papers in order of priority, with the most important task on top.

Next step: Take the three top items and give each one to a friend. Explain to your friend what you want to accomplish within the next 30 days. Ask him to call several times a week to check up on your progress. (A little encouragement wouldn't hurt either.) As you concentrate on those three areas, keep a record of your progress as well.

9
A Feeling of Worth

A North Dakota couple had it all planned. During the long, cold winter evenings they would often sit at the kitchen table in snowbound Fargo and, over a second cup of coffee, sketch out their vacation routes in a well-thumbed Rand-McNally road atlas.

Key to their enjoyment of Northern California would be a lazy week in a rented houseboat on beautiful Lake Shasta. Nestled in the rugged foothills of the Siskiyou Mountains, this lovely lake grew ever bluer and more serene in their memories as the Midwestern winter wind gnawed at the storm windows.

In the meantime, however, a persistent Northern California drought had been sending what remained of Lake Shasta over the gates of the dam and down the Sacramento River to aid the beleaguered vegetable farmers of the lower valley. We need not register the expressions of the North Dakota pilgrims when they at last reached the threshold of their dream lake to find it had become a rather unsightly brown puddle in a yawning rocky crater.

You have a reservoir in your life. Planted at its edge is a sign which reads: Lake Self-Esteem. When the reservoir is filled, there is a wide-reaching serenity that laps a hundred shores, and a great depth of joy and satisfaction which gives calmness, hue and beauty.

Surging over the floodgates is a constant flow of productivity bringing life and help to many others. You have confidence and are looking forward to whatever challenge life may bring.

The ability you have to produce, to be constructive, will always be influenced by the view you have of yourself. When your reservoir of self-esteem is low, you will find it difficult to move ahead with confidence. Looking out across the shallow puddle where a lake belongs, you are vulnerable to feelings of doubt and insecurity. "Can it be done? What if I fail? I'd better not launch out. I'd better stay anchored where I am, even though I know I'm getting a little stagnant."

Previous bad experiences hold us back. We've risked before once or twice and failed. Rather than being burned again, it is much easier to rest in well-established habits of life and play it safe. New challenges, new friendships, new ministries are out of the question. The old ways, the old routines are less threatening and infinitely more comfortable. Still . . . there is that vague feeling of discontent—that inner something that wistfully regrets a missed opportunity and silently dreads an extended anchorage in a rut. The voice that says, "Hey, I'm growing nowhere. Life is going by. Is there more? Is this all there is?"

Is there a way out of the rut? This chapter is written to help you establish a greater feeling of worth. As you fill the reservoir of self-esteem, you will be able to approach living in new ways that will be adventuresome and rewarding.

The reservoir of self-esteem is filled from three sources. One source splashes in like a stream from outside while the other two sources flow from deep inner springs.

When you are valued by others for who you are as well as for what you do, the supply of worth is replenished. This is the outside input which is so vital and necessary to maintain the level of the reservoir.

Fathoms underneath, the two inner springs are also vital. First of all, self-esteem is enhanced when you try something new and succeed. The reward of success builds confidence to be creative in still other ways. Realizing that you are a unique individual, you bring a contribution to life out of that inner spring of esteem that no one else can bring.

But perhaps the greatest of all sources of self-worth is a source that is available only to those who have trusted Jesus Christ. We will examine this vast "underground" undergirding river a little bit later, seeing why the Christian's reservoir of self-esteem should brim over its banks and generate great amounts of productive energy for the tasks which life presents.

How many people do you know who will not respond to a warm, heartfelt word of appreciation? Probably few. What a feeling of elation to have a friend say, "Terrific job! You've really accomplished something important and I value you more because of what you've done!" We respond to that sort of comment—our reservoir level goes up a little. Yet, that is not enough.

Sandra felt depressed. She was a good wife and mother. Her husband had no complaints. She was a good housekeeper. Meals in the home were on schedule and nourishing. The children were kept clean and were not neglected. The husband and wife had a good sexual relationship. Sandra was thrifty; she managed the household budget well.

Why was she depressed? Her life had become routine. Sandra felt she was valued only for what she did, not for *who she was.* She needed her husband to love her just for being Sandra, not because she was a good wife or mother.

It is important not to get the cart before the horse. Your feeling of worth is not increased through external duties, however multiplied or important they may be. You are not more worthwhile because of what you do. It is because you do *have* internal worth that you give evidence of that intrinsic quality in the way you live. *The inner person flows out in the outward act.* It is only when you realize that you are capable and highly valued that you choose to live productively.

What provides us the freedom to build on this inner strength? Essentially, it is the ability to accept responsibility for our own actions. The right to choose and to live with the consequences of that choice develops the resources from within.

A mother called me at the community college and asked me to see her son. Without consulting his parents, Jim had dropped out the third quarter of his junior year in high school, and had enrolled in three courses at the community college. But it wasn't long before he was demonstrating an inability to handle the freedom of the community college setting. His failure to attend classes had resulted in a failing grade for each of the three courses. Becoming aware of the situation, the parents were growing increasingly alarmed, and the mother had called the counselor to request help for her son.

Jim's parents were both successful in business ventures. The mother held a responsible position as an executive in a marketing firm, while the father managed a corporation with more than sixty employees directly accountable to him. But in terms of their son's development, things weren't progressing according to plan at all. Wanting Jim to be successful, the parents were greatly disappointed with his apparent lack of progress.

In our first session, I asked Jim what he wanted to do in the future, and the reply seemed confident enough: "I think I'd like to be an architect."

In an effort to be helpful, we scheduled a second appointment. During that time I carefully showed Jim what courses he could take at the community college to finish the credits needed to complete high school and at the same time be building a good preparation for architectural training. An enthusiastic Jim signed up for the recommended courses to begin in the fall. As a further incentive, I asked Jim to stop by every two weeks to let the counselor know how things were going. For the first six weeks things appeared to go well. Then Jim failed to stop by. Records revealed that he had not been attending classes.

Again the parents came to me for help. This time we set up a plan for Jim to work on a special high school graduation program. Again the plan failed.

The situation had me puzzled. What was wrong? These were good plans—carefully considered and tailored to meet Jim's needs. Why had they failed? Jim was capable. He appeared to get along well with others. Why couldn't he stick with the program?

I decided to go to lunch with the father to see if I could understand the dynamics of Jim's difficulties a little better. Out of this discussion over lunch I saw for the first time how little opportunity Jim had had to be responsible for his own decisions. In their efforts to "help Jim along," his parents had carefully engineered his life for him since diaper days. At that point, it hit me that I had simply been contributing to Jim's growing sense of despair. I had been doing the same thing as Jim's parents—taking away Jim's sense of responsibility by trying to tell him what to do.

In the next session, I made up my mind to take a completely new approach. Instead of methodically charting Jim's next steps, I determined to create a climate where Jim was free to make his own decisions and to live with the consequences of his choice. The session lasted more than two hours. Jim made three decisions.

First, he decided that he could and would get himself up in the morning. Often in the past when he had had a fight with his parents, they failed to call him in the morning. As a result, he would get up too late to attend classes.

Second, Jim would tell his parents when he wasn't going to go to school. He was now eighteen. Previously when he was taken to school, if he didn't want to attend classes, he would walk in the front door and out the back.

Third, when he went to his independent study classes, he would only stay as long as he could keep his attention on his work. He would not allow himself to daydream. When he finished studying, he would leave for the day.

The three decisions were hard-fought, and Jim toiled over each of them. It would have been much easier for me simply to sketch them out and hand them down to the counselee. At the close of the session, Jim started to cry. He looked at me, shook his head, then suddenly looked up and blurted out, "You're the first person who ever really understood me."

What had I done? Simply enhanced Jim's self-esteem. My attitude said, "Jim, you are a person of worth. You have the ability to choose your own trail, make your own decisions, or at least some of them. I support you in that right."

How do parents transmit to their children a growing sense of responsibility? If the child is asked to make too many decisions too early in life, he or she feels abandoned. "No one cares," he feels. "No one will help me."

It is like being asked to descend a narrow mountain pass with no guardrails in a car with the throttle stuck at fifty miles an hour. Life descends too quickly, decisions too important loom too rapidly. There is fear.

If, on the other hand, all decisions are made for the child, he or she feels no sense of freedom. Life becomes an air-conditioned tour bus ride. Beckoning roads and inviting vistas are left behind as the tour guide rushes along on his predetermined route according to his preplanned schedule playing prerecorded music and reading from a prepared script. There is no opportunity for the child to explore, to make mistakes, to try again—to grow. No opportunity to develop a sense of uniqueness and worth.

As you make the decisions to try new approaches to living, you gain confidence when those decisions work out well. It is a cycle. The reservoir of self-esteem is filled when you try something new and succeed. This in turn gives you the confidence to try again. You again try something new which gives a greater feeling of worth, and on the process goes.

If your decisions fail to work as planned, discouragement sets in. Failure diminishes your supply of self-esteem and makes you reluctant to risk again. The level of esteem in the reservoir changes according to how much flows in from the stream and the two inner springs in contrast to how much is lost through seepage or evaporation due to failures.

When the failures outnumber the successes, you find it

hard to pour yourself into something new. Yet, the irony of this situation is that the less you move ahead into new challenges, the less will be your feeling of worth. In this reservoir, outflow over the floodgates is required before the inflow of fresh self-esteem can replenish the lake. Sometimes it seems like a trap. We seem doomed to drought.

As we cut back our outflow of productive activities to avoid failure and conserve our self-esteem, the input of encouragement from friends and from our own growing confidence decreases proportionately.

But here the hidden spring comes into play. We are highly valued and esteemed by God.

> By this the love of God was manifested in us, that God has sent His only begotten Son into the world, so that we might live through Him (I John 4:9).

> See how great a love the Father has bestowed upon us, that we should be called children of God; and such we are . . . (I John 3:1).

Another paraphrase of this latter verse suggests that our heredity on the Godward side is no mere figure of speech. You are loved of God! Not for what you can do, nor what you can produce, nor for how you can perform—but for yourself! God loves you because it is His nature to love and He has chosen to freely bestow that love upon you.

> How precious also are Thy thoughts to me, O God! How vast is the sum of them! If I should count them, they would outnumber the sand. When I awake, I am still with Thee (Psalm 139:17-18).

As Christians, we are children of God. Our sins are forgiven. Guilt is gone. We have been drawn into His family circle. As we believe and practice these incredible truths, our reservoir of self-esteem is filled to capacity and will spill over into many new channels of growth and productivity.

> For we are His workmanship, created in Christ Jesus for good works, which God prepared beforehand, that we should walk in them (Ephesians 2:10).

In the same way that a parent builds a sense of responsibility into his or her children, so likewise God builds patiently in the life of that person who has trusted in Him. Does not God give to each of us the opportunity to make decisions and to live with the consequences of our choice?

Yet we are not abandoned. God provides the safety and security of a wise and loving Father. He defines the limits and keeps us from straying too far.

But living the life of a Christian is more still. Granted access into the very presence of God, we develop the skill of negotiating with God. As between father and child, this requires open communication in a nonthreatening atmosphere of trust. Listening to God through His Word, the Bible, and talking to Him through prayer lead us to effective, productive living.

And so our lake ripples full and serene, even as the force of the overflow generates power to warm cold corners and light darkened windows.

INTERACTION #9

Take a few minutes to apply the thoughts expressed in this chapter to the subject of raising children.

Maybe you've already raised them. Maybe you're not a parent. Maybe you're not even married. That's okay. Feel free to participate. As you do, you may want to focus in on these questions:

1) How do we teach responsibility?

2) How is a feeling of worth related to performance?

3) Am I a worthwhile person if I perform badly?

4) Does God love me when I do wrong?

5) What advantages or disadvantages do you see in parental authority as opposed to individual accountability?

10
A Goal to Be Gained

We've all pictured ourselves in that future rocking chair, creaking back and forth, asking questions of a life almost spent. We've all talked to older people whose lives are as filled with bitterness and regret as driftwood is with sea-salt.

"If only I had ... if only I could have ... if only ... if only. ..." And the rocking chair creaks on.

No! No, we say. My life will be different—special—like no other life before. God forbid that I wake up at age 65 and see that my years were foolishly invested in valueless trinkets and baubles. God keep me from the might-have-been, should-have-been rocking chair.

What is it that will make my life one that has been worth living? It must be the realization that somehow *my life has made a difference.* Although history books, sculptors and songwriters may scarcely note my passing, I want to approach that moment with the inner assurance that others have been encouraged by my example, challenged by my achievement, or touched by my care.

It is not the knowledge of approaching death that makes the rocking chair unendurable; it is the knowledge of a wasted potential. How can I insure that this will not occur? How can I really begin to become all that God wants me to be? My contribution to living will largely depend on the goals I have set for the future.

The mind balks at looking ahead sometimes. Fear and uncertainties roll in like fog from the ocean and cloud our perspective. "What if . . .?" hangs heavy on the horizon.

But how foolish and self-defeating it would be to allow our fear of the future to keep us from plotting a course and setting goals for our lives. Life *is* the future.

If the captain of a ship never bothered to map out a course, what would keep him from spending his life sailing in circles around the harbor? A goal is that which lifts the human life from the animal level of simply meeting biological needs and gives it a direction, a will, the force of desire and the elation of achievement.

Imagine how ridiculous athletic contests would become if the goals were removed. Picture yourself shelling out $7.50 to watch professional basketball players demonstrate their talents on a court with no basket. Plays may be executed brilliantly—like a well-oiled machine. Passes may be fired like bull's-eye pistol shots at a wild West show, but you want your money back. Why? Without a goal, the game has simply become a meaningless drill.

Consider a football game with no first down markers and no goalposts. The quarterback would call the play; the team would break the huddle, execute the play, and come back for the next one. When one team had done three or four plays, the other team would get its turn, and back and forth the activity would go on. Where would be the incentive if you couldn't score?

Skaters on the ice fight madly to control the direction of the puck. Referees are there to enforce the rules of hockey. Yet bedlam reigns, for someone has failed to put red lines or blue lines on the ice and the scoring cages are nowhere in sight. The chaotic confusion of unceasing activity in a directionless arena offers little attraction to the participant or to the spectator.

The tennis match has been underway for five hours. One slight change has been instituted in the scoring procedure. Games will be counted, but sets will not. Presently one player has won 53 games, the other player 52 games. The fans left the bleachers several hours ago. The players appear uncertain as to whether they should go on.

Other examples undoubtedly come to your mind. What would happen to golf if there were no cups or greens; to chess if there were no checkmate, or to poker if there were no pot?

Can you afford to be in the stream of life without knowing where you are going? The confusion of having so many things to accomplish, so many directions in which to move becomes debilitating when there is no goal that gives focus and clarity to your activities. Not only is it confusing to you, but it is also frustrating for those deeply-concerned spectators on the sidelines of your life who witness aimless efforts and futile activity instead of progress toward a meaningful objective.

We do not live as unto ourselves; everyone of us has a circle of "watchers." When our life becomes little more than aimless effort, there are younger ones and weaker ones looking on who become discouraged and lose heart in their own swim against the current.

Although it seems difficult to believe, the greatest contribution and impact that we may produce in the lives of others is to be a person who makes steady progress toward our own goals. As we move, stroke by stoke, upstream toward the objective that fills our vision, water-treaders and downstream drifters may be given new heart and a second wind to achieve goals of their own.

Have you heard someone say, "If it's important, it will happen no matter what you do; so don't worry about it. If it's supposed to happen, it will; and if it's not, it won't, regardless of what you do or say"?

Such a fatalistic attitude encourages an early surrender to the circumstances in life, a cessation of progress, and deformity rather than growth. It is true that certain things in life are beyond a person's control; yet, not all things fall into that category. It would be foolish to lie down on a railroad track and say, "Oh well, if my life is meant to be spared, the train won't run over me." We are responsible for those things we can control.

It is true that there are many facets of our life that were simply given to us. We cannot change the fact that we are either a man or a woman, short or tall, a bass or a tenor, dark or fair, but we have been entrusted with the priceless possession called life. And further, we know that the One who bestowed that gift upon us expects gain from our life—worthwhile investment of the potential that He has given us.

The process of conscious growth begins by selecting a goal worthy of your energy. Goals may be set that pertain to any dimension of your life but goals should be worked on one at a time.

Some questions to illustrate a few goals might prompt you to consider other goals more applicable to your situation.

Financial Goals:
a. What level of income is desired?
b. What type of house would I want?
c. What worthwhile charities do I support?
d. What amount is necessary for proper attire?
e. What level of security is necessary for retirement years?

Physical Goals:
a. What weight should I maintain?
b. What exercise should become a part of the daily routine?
c. What number of hours should be given to work?
d. How many hours of sleep are desired?
e. What diet will give the best results?

Spiritual Goals:
a. How much time should be devoted to personal study and prayer?
b. Should I be working more or less in the church?
c. How can I practice in daily life the principles I learn?
d. Are there methods to help others in their spiritual growth?
e. How can I evaluate my growth?

Social Goals:	a.	Which people do I want to know better?
	b.	How often should I visit or have people over?
	c.	What social organizations should I join?
	d.	How can I tell people what I think without turning them off?
	e.	What do I do to let people know that I really care about them?

Recreational Goals:	a.	How often do I want to dine out?
	b.	What recreational activities do I enjoy?
	c.	What social goals can be met through these activities?
	d.	What purpose is fulfilled through my recreation?
	e.	Are other areas uncared for if I do what I want to recreationally?

Many other questions could be asked in each area and certainly more goals could be suggested. To start, you must select one area and ask yourself, "What do I want to accomplish in this area of my life? What is important to me?"

As you begin to ask questions, some answers will be forthcoming. At that point, it is necessary to take inventory of your assets. What is necessary to achieve the goals you have set? An example of a mountain climber will illustrate the point.

What do you do if you choose to climb a mountain? Start by selecting which mountain is worthy of your efforts. Remember, you only climb one mountain at a time. Have you adequate equipment to scale the rocks or repel the cliffs? Are you properly dressed for the winds and temperatures which may be faced? Is there sufficient food and water for the journey? Have you charted the course and built in stopping points to evaluate the climb on the way?

What resources are available to you to achieve the outcome which you desire? Be realistic. It is not possible to climb a mountain when the pack on your back is too heavy, or you haven't brought along proper equipment for the task. Build in some check stations along the way. How are you doing? Are you at the place you had planned to be at this time? What adjustments are necessary before starting out on the next leg of the journey?

Don't try to accomplish too much too quickly. It takes time and effort to achieve a worthwhile goal. Chances are you will trip and fall several times before you achieve the level you are seeking. Don't be discouraged. Get up and get going again. Remember, it's important to achieve that goal. When you realize that you are almost there, that the goal has almost been met, you will want to set a higher goal, for now you know how to climb the mountain and get where you are going.

The central motivating goal in the life of the Apostle Paul was to ". . . know Him [Christ], and the power of His resurrection . . ." (Philippians 3:10).

Paul quickly followed that remark with an explanation lest his readers get the idea that he was some sort of "super saint" who couldn't relate to the struggle of swimming upstream. The apostle made no pretense of perfection. He realized that there was a long way to go. However, he wanted to establish a definite goal and then put his energy into achieving that aim.

Working hard in life is not enough. The captain worked hard trimming his sails as his ship cruised clockwise circles in the harbor. Though he might sail for years in that pattern, logging mile after mile until the sails were threadbare and the planks on the deck rotted away, he still *wasn't going anywhere.* You must have a goal!

But then, neither is merely having a goal enough. Hitler had a goal to crush the peoples of the world under his thumb. Others have had the goal to make money or to acquire the adulation of thousands.

Make certain that when you chart your course for a faraway island your arrival years later will not reveal a barren pile of rocks in the midst of a lonely sea.

Is your goal worthy of your life?

INTERACTION #10

Thumb back through this chapter for a second look at the questions on financial, physical, spiritual, social and recreational goals. Try making up a similar questionnaire and administer it to four of your friends.

How well have your friends defined these goals in their life? How could you encourage them to be more specific in their answers?

PART THREE:
The Fine Art of Swimming Upstream

Travelers overseas usually carry at least one other item in addition to their passports and digestive medications. It's an invaluable little device which fits neatly into the palm of the hand. Properly employed, it has the power to take something useless and potentially destructive and transform it into something unfailingly helpful and thoroughly usable. Transform is a good word because that's what it is: a transformer.

Plugged into a wall socket of the high voltage European electrical systems, the handy transformer enables American visitors to use their low voltage shavers, radios, hair dryers and curling irons without melting their appliances into the Old World floorboards.

Without that humming little helper, all the electricity in Europe would not serve to shave a single whisker or iron a single curl.

What if there was a transformer for the heat and pressure of everyday living? What if someone could invent a way to take all the negatives and positives that constantly bombard our lives and plug them into a device that could make the pressure helpful and usable? If we could only gain from our pain—grow through our struggle. Maybe we can.

Perhaps a process could be learned and practiced which could help us convert our experience of struggle and pain into an experience of growth. Such a process might prove costly; transformers may not be cheap. But then, neither is life. Possessing something infinitely valuable gives us the responsibility of learning to make it work productively.

11
Maintaining Balance

From his expression, you'd think he had just conquered Everest. The ten-month-old baby pulls himself up onto his feet, fingers clinging to the davenport. Baby's big grin displays a profound sense of accomplishment. After tottering for a moment on this dizzy summit, progress is lost when, with a sudden plunk, the infant takes a seat on the carpet. After a few tears, he's at it again, wobbling like a drunken sailor, beaming broadly over each new triumph.

In what seems like a few days, the baby is charging down the hallway or waddling full throttle across the back yard. Progress has not been without bumps and bruises, but the little one has mastered the secret. He has learned how to balance the weight of his body on two small feet.

Five years later, that same child might be observed on a fencetop, gingerly stepping from post to post. With arms extended like airplane wings and tongue fixed firmly between the teeth, the daredevil amazes his friends and alarms his mother as he develops his skills. Forward motion is a painstaking process, slowed further by occasional nose dives. But before long, it's easier. Even without the help of the tongue and airplane wings. Even at a jog. The child has gained a level of proficiency in maintaining balance. If you were a therapist studying intricacies of the balancing process you would be awed by the complex set of factors involved in maintaining equilibrium. But for the kid on the fence, "Hey, it's easy! I've got it down!"

Try handing the fence-walker a bucket of apples. Ask him to walk on the wall while holding the full bucket at arm's length to one side. Now what happens to the confident aerial artist? Most likely child, apples and bucket will immediately form a small heap on the turf. It is like learning to balance all over again. Obviously, more practice would be required to make that sort of adjustment and keep one's balance on the fencetop.

Carry the picture to an extreme, if you will, to make a point. Imagine that the child is required to carry the bulging apple bucket all of his waking hours each day. Everywhere he goes and everything he does—there's that pail in his right hand. Before long you'd expect the poor kid to be constantly leaning to the left in order to compensate for the weight of the apples. After a month of this activity, he might develop a permanent "tilt" as he walked. At that point, if you relieved him of his burden he would most likely collapse. He would need that tub of fruit to maintain balance. Removing it would require another adjustment in balancing skill.

In a sense, we're all fence-walkers. Life is a process of learning balance. Healthy growth requires an understanding of the components of our makeup, and then the ability to develop each component proportionately to maintain balance. If one part of us grows rapidly while other components are not growing at all, then balance is destroyed. Like the child with the apple bucket, life grows at a "tilt," rather than evenly.

But what's inside these buckets? What components make us the kind of people we are becoming? What ingredients give us the potential for balance in the onrushing current of daily living? First, there are the things we know, secondly, there are the things we feel; and thirdly, there are the things we decide to do.

Each area or component has an interdependence with the other two areas. What we know or think will influence how we feel and will be observed by others through what we decide to do. If one area is indulged while another area is deprived, one part of us shrivels while another part grows overweight. Healthy growth requires balanced distribution in the three buckets.

If I pour myself into the pursuit of intellectual trophies to the exclusion of other areas of life, I'm tilted—unbalanced. If I spend my free hours in the cultivation of certain emotional experiences, ignoring other priorities, I'm still tilting. If my calendar is choked with a dense smog of activities so that I am too busy to reflect on my thoughts and feelings, I'm walking with one foot in the ditch. I'm listing to port or starboard like a sailboat in a typhoon. The well-balanced person develops each area of life proportionately. Sending roots into three different areas the tree resists unsettling winds and matures straight toward the sun.

DIAGRAM TEN

BALANCED GROWTH

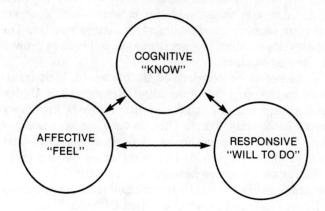

To focus attention on one or two areas without giving equal attention to the remaining will cause you to grow out of balance. Each of the three areas is important and needs to be enhanced simultaneously.

It is not possible to separate one area from the other two; i.e., your thinking is interlocked with how you feel and what you do.

Your thinking and feelings are revealed to others in what you do.

What about the bucket we call the mind? How long has it been since you've considered upgrading its contents? What do you spend your time thinking about? Is there anything fresh or stimulating in the bucket which might challenge you toward more productive living? Perhaps the contents have grown a little stagnant.

Our bucket fills rapidly and not always in the way we would desire. Between television and the daily onslaught of Madison Avenue, it can be rather amazing to glance into the bucket and see what's accumulated.

Slip your car into neutral and if it isn't guided it might roll anywhere, doing damage to itself and to other vehicles. Similarly, how can a person be responsible if he or she does not think about what is being done? Can you feel good about yourself if you don't accept responsibility for what you do? Are you accountable for actions which generate from your thoughts and feelings? Of course you are! The underdeveloped mind is a great danger to positive growth and adequate balance.

We are not to be "conformed to this world," but transformed by the renewing of our mind (Romans 12:2). Understanding begins in the mind and filters its way into every aspect of everyday living. This, in turn, creates positive feelings of confidence within us. A basis of meaning—that which we know—is provided for what we do. We are given credibility as we are recognized as "thinking" people. A profitable exercise would be to check all the imperatives in the Bible which tell us what we should "*know.*"

As important as it is to continually renew our minds, that is to think, this activity alone will not produce balanced growth. Knowledge without feeling is sterile. Knowledge without application is wasted. Knowledge is growth-producing only when it modifies what you do and how you feel.

Jesus spent a very long day with a great, pressing crowd of people. Hours slipped by. Many were fascinated and awed by His teaching. Still others were healed of lifelong diseases. But shadows were lengthening and the sun seemed to be disappearing into the golden water on the far side of the Sea of Galilee.

It was a desolate spot, and there wasn't a market for miles. Jesus knew the people were very hungry. As He considered the situation, the Teacher felt a surge of compassion for the throng. As an outgrowth of His love, Jesus took five loaves and two fish and provided enough food to feed the multitude of five thousand men plus women and children. Notice the progression here. What Jesus *knew* made a difference in how Jesus *felt* which resulted in what Jesus *did.*

Duane was an excellent student. He had one of the highest grade point averages in the seminary's graduating class. In view of Duane's superior scholarship, several churches invited him to candidate for a position as senior pastor. When a call came from one of those churches, Duane and his wife accepted. From the very first Sunday, Duane's skill in sermon-craft was clearly evident. Hours of careful preparation and exhaustive study gave the young minister a unique ability to teach the Bible with clarity and precision.

Duane lasted three years in the pastorate. Today he is in another profession. The church rolls registered zero growth during the three years Duane and his wife were there. Thinking God had let him down, Duane left the ministry a frustrated man.

What went wrong? Why was Duane unsuccessful in the task for which he had so diligently trained? People in the church would tell you, "Oh, he was a fine preacher, but he just didn't have a pastor's heart. He didn't know how to relate to people. It was really a struggle for him to express love, care, or concern. We could feel it."

Duane had learned the things he was to know and some of the things he was to do; but unfortunately, he had not learned how to respond to feelings within himself or to the feelings of others. His congregation was more than a collection of minds, more than a gathering of intellects to be probed and prodded. They were people—many of them with aching emotional needs as well as knowledge gaps.

Duane poured so much into one bucket that the echo from the empty ones became deafening. A potentially dynamic ministry was lost because a pattern of unbalanced growth was revealed under fire.

Feelings are important. As mentioned earlier, feelings are to be acted on, not bottled up. All emotions are God-given and can be used to help us to grow. It's not wrong to feel angry, nor to be afraid. These emotions can be as beneficial as feelings of love or joy. Feelings become self-destructive when they fail to meet two conditions: *First, feelings should be based on sound thinking; and second, feelings should result in responsible action.*

Unless these conditions are met, feelings do not contribute to balanced growth.

Have you ever seen someone roll pious eyes to heaven and say, "I don't *know* why I did it. I just felt like I should." The "spiritual" tone of voice reveals a smug, self-satisfied conviction that bypassing the gray matter represents a sort of moral triumph. This is an attitude expressed freely today. People are seeking an experience, a feeling in which to luxuriate. Too often, they check their brains out during the quest.

Monogrammed T-shirts advise, "If it feels good, do it." Advertisements suggest, "You only go around once, so grab all the gusto you can."

These expressions suggest that a selfish hedonism will bring happiness. Many would testify that such is not the case.

A society that indulges feelings which are not based on sound thinking soon loses its values. Any principle can be compromised in a group which permits the individual to indulge any feeling, rational or not. Masquerading in the garb of freedom, feeling may become the most vicious dictator of all.

How then does a person experience and express feelings in a growth-producing way? Suppose a couple comes to you for counseling. They have been married for fifteen years but now they are ready to pull the plug. Divorce is dark and murky on the horizon. The man and woman have been separated for a month. The wife is keeping the three children.

In the counseling sessions you attempt to unravel the throbbing knot of feelings which has brought the marriage to the brink of death. The wife is saturated with bitterness toward her husband. For years she has suppressed feelings of dismay and anger when she felt her husband had wronged her. The differences were never discussed, let alone resolved, and now her list of wrongs is a cancer that gorges itself on the remaining tissues of tenderness and mutual respect in the relationship. Feelings have been left to fester rather than being confronted and healed.

The husband has detected a certain coldness on the part of his wife. She has not responded warmly to his love-making efforts for some time and he feels rejected. Again, he has let the matter slide so that he no longer tries to display affection toward his wife. The wound in the marriage is spray-painted with apathy and the infection spreads.

Still the situation is not hopeless. The husband and wife have each invested fifteen years in this marriage. And it's more than years they have deposited in one another's accounts—it's life. There have been moments of closeness, spontaneous outpourings of affection. Joys, struggles, laughter, heartaches, accomplishments, and setbacks have all formed a part of the rich relationship they have shared together for a decade and a half.

But now the disease runs deep. How can healing begin? The wife will need to forgive her husband, give up the list of wrongs, erase the board and begin again. As she does, she will need to develop confrontive and constructive ways to resolve her feelings when she is angry with her husband, rather than locking those feelings inside herself.

The husband will need to learn effective ways to express love toward his wife, ways that communicate his care and concern for her. It won't be easy. Mistakes and painful setbacks will be part of the process. It will require time for the relationship to mend.

Sound thinking says it's worth it, so the couple work toward reconciliation. Husband and wife each accept responsibility to make the marriage viable. Though it's expensive to continue in counseling, a commitment is made to do so. Progress is precious and the investments too costly to risk. Both want to build for the future. It will require the right balance of thought, feeling and willful action.

INTERACTION #11

All of us recognize the strength of feeling. All of us have done things we felt like doing even though we knew better.

If we are ever to experience the thrill of seeing conscious change in our lives, we must learn the strength of choosing. A cognitive process. In spite of our feelings. This is a learned skill and it isn't easy. But success helps. As we achieve proficiency, the ability to discipline feelings through conscious choice begins to increase.

Try it. Take one thing you really like to do but know you shouldn't. Write down all the rational observations you can think of as to why you should change in this particular area. When you are fully persuaded in your own mind to discontinue this behavior, determine (will) to stop it.

Remember, don't try to tackle a major reconstruction process. Work on one behavior. One. When the time comes for you to move on to another area, you'll be working from a firm platform.

12
The Blessedness
of Struggle

"Has it hit you? The children are raised."

"Just a couple more years 'til retirement."

"Then the pace is gonna change."

"Right. We'll have time to relax a little."

"Time to do some of the things we've always wanted to do."

Don and Martha looked across the supper table at one another, trying to gather enough energy to get up and clear the table. Both of them dreamed of some breathing room in the next few years. Thoughts of retirement and travel seemed like a well-deserved dessert after years of long hours and heavy schedules.

Neither of them anticipated their daughter's divorce. Neither of them foresaw two little boys left without adequate parental care. Grandma and Grandpa were compelled to assume the duties of parents to their grandchildren. The adjustment wasn't easy. So many things to do. Instead of gearing down, Martha and Don were now busier than ever. There was always a wash to be done, a meal to fix or somewhere the boys needed to be taken.

Was it really fair? They'd already raised one family. Was it right to expect them to raise another one? Bitter thoughts that floated to the surface had to be dismissed or resubmerged. The little guys needed them now.

Martha's mother and father were reaching that age where it was getting harder and harder to manage for themselves. Somewhere in the day a couple of hours had to be carved for Martha to clean up their house, fix them a meal and see how they were doing. Trips to the doctor, trips to the store, trips to the bank—it all took time.

Don and Martha were amazed at their own ability to cope. A few years back they had thought life was as complicated as it could become; they hadn't seen anything yet. Sometimes as they passed one another at high gear in the hallway their eyes would meet for a moment. Would life ever allow breathing room? Were there any quiet little corners in their future?

It's easy for many of us to identify with Don and Martha's plight. Sometimes rush hour lasts all day. Cruising space is at a premium as bumper-to-bumper events crowd and claw for room on a six-lane schedule. So much to do and so little time to do it. And what can be cut? Everything's important, right?

Sometimes the pressure feels so oppressive it seems as though you can't go on. Your eyes search in vain for an exit lane. In the back of your mind you wonder, "Why does God permit these circumstances? It isn't fair. He knows I can't handle all this pressure right now."

The Apostle Paul once described a similar feeling in his own life:

> For we do not want you to be unaware, brethren, of our affliction which came to us in Asia, that we were burdened excessively, beyond our strength, so that we despaired even of life; indeed, we had the sentence of death within ourselves in order that we should not trust in ourselves, but in God who raises the dead; who delivered us from so great a peril of death, and will deliver us, He on whom we have set our hope. And He will yet deliver us (II Corinthians 1:8-10).

The pressure Paul describes is pictured by a man lying on his back. Heavy stones are heaped on the man's chest until life itself is squeezed out of him. It's the despair that says, "I can't go on. The demands of living are more than I can take."

Our pace becomes our tyrant to the point that we lose our perspective. We forget that each struggle provides an opportunity for growth. Coping with the pressures of each day can actually provide new strength. God provides the resources necessary to accomplish what He desires and requires of our lives. Too often we ask for relief when we need to pray for strength.

When a walnut orchard reaches a certain age, limbs are pruned back while shoots from high-producing varieties are carefully grafted into the trunk and major limbs. If it is a good graft, it may grow very rapidly, perhaps as much as ten or twelve feet in the first summer. These fast-growing grafts break very easily in the first year or two. A few birds deciding to perch on a solid-looking grafted limb can break the whole thing right out of the trunk and send it crashing to the ground. Or a wind may come up, tearing out the graft.

Realizing that his young grafts can be so easily damaged or destroyed, the farmer will often nail a board to the trunk alongside the graft. As it grows, the graft is tied with something pliable—a nylon stocking is good—to the supporting brace. The board may be left for two or three years, until the graft is strong enough to withstand the wind and other perils on its own. At that time the farmer can remove the board. The graft has enough strength to stand on its own without a brace.

What is it that gives the vitality to the graft to withstand the wind? It is the wind itself. Do you see the great paradox? As the graft, with the help of the brace, resists the pressure of the wind, it gains strength until it is able to withstand the wind on its own.

Let's apply the same principle to our own daily hurricane. Sometimes as we lean into the wind, the pressure becomes too great for us to weather alone. We cry for help to God or to a close friend and that person comes alongside to provide the support necessary to get us through the struggle. As this process is repeated, we develop the character to face greater pressure, to work our way through stiffer storms.

127

Without struggle we would develop little strength for our remaining years. Adversity enables us to develop and utilize our resources. And those resources are awesome, beyond comprehension. Wiring ourselves to a dozen nuclear power plants would be a pale comparison to tapping the eternal energy of our Almighty God:

Finally, be strong in the Lord, and in the strength of His might (Ephesians 6:10).

Run that verse through your computer one more time. Paul's plea is that Christians consider their power source. Inevitably, we are only willing to plug into the vast voltage of the "mainline" after we've exhausted our own little half-watted penlight batteries. Standing in the fog of daily pressures we realize our weak little beam is insufficient to illuminate the path. So we call in God's mighty searchlight. And step on ahead. And begin to grow.

The most difficult struggles seem to come when we are least prepared for them. It is the unexpected which invades life so pretentiously and with such poor timing. Just when we seem to be squeezing the last puzzle pieces into place someone storms in and kicks the table over.

Consider a family that has had financial struggles. Bills flock to the mailbox like robins to a cherry tree. Careful planning has enabled the family to cut down on expenditures and for a few weeks it looks like the paycheck might come close to covering the month's demands. Then a tidal wave thunders in. An unexpected illness comes into the family which is not covered by insurance, resulting in astronomical doctor and hospital bills. For all their careful planning, the family is rewarded with apparent disaster.

We've all faced it in one way or another. This business of taking one step upstream makes a nice theme, but the *process* seems to be almost brutal sometimes. We lose our footing on a slimy rock and fall backwards in the current. The water surges cold, and fresh bruises ache with merciless intensity.

But we struggle upright again, regain our balance and slog ahead once more. Of course, not all of life is slogging and struggling, but make a list of ten worthwhile achievements which you've accomplished in the last five years. Were any of them achieved without struggle? Has growth in any area of life ever been easy? It is the process of struggling which builds determination, confidence and still greater strength.

Can you expect to glide toward your upstream destination with effortless ease? No, it will most likely demand great effort, great faith, and a realization that the uncharted stream ahead may contain surprises.

Knowing that deep holes and half-hidden rocks lie ahead is an encouragement to keep your eyes trained on the next step. Looking back and moving ahead are highly incompatible activities. A preoccupation with the past tends to cancel progress toward any goal. While the mind tells us that it is impossible to undo that which is already done, the emotions often try to punish us for missteps and wrong turns. How many hours have been spent fretting over: "If I just hadn't done that . . . I feel so rotten when I let myself do those things."

Tuned into this wavelength, it's easy for discouragement to drift in and suggest that we give up rather than struggle. True, the past is inescapable, but it should be used to help us on our way rather than snarl our feet like briers. A right attitude toward our past can elevate us to a useful perspective. Examining the present in the light of the past, we are able to plan wisely for the future.

Imagine a farmer pruning his orchard. In the afternoon he brings out a pot of glue and returns to several trees he had pruned earlier in the morning. On each tree he finds a limb that he had cut off by mistake, so he spends painstaking hours gluing each limb back on the tree right where he cut it off. You know, it doesn't really matter how careful and conscientious the farmer is. The limb will not grow. No way. No chance. It's done. When a limb is cut off a tree, it is not possible to mend the situation hours later by gluing the limb back. The farmer has to live with the fact that the limb has been cut off the tree and the tree will have to grow on without the limb.

Hopefully, however, the farmer will learn from his mistake and will not continue to cut off needed limbs as he goes about the rest of the pruning. He examines the tree he is presently working on in the light of the mistake he made earlier, and decides what limbs should be pruned on the remaining trees. He examines the present in the light of the past to plan for the future.

People who put themselves down often do so by bringing up the past. Do you know any people like this? You find that their lives are walking apologies. Feelings of incompetence are continually indulged. The result is confusion, depression, and misery on their part. On your part, you'd just as soon walk three blocks out of your way to avoid them.

Remember the last chapter? A feeling should be indulged only if: 1) it is based on sound thinking; and 2) it results in responsible action. Action is in the future, so this sadistic love affair with broken limbs is not healthy. The put-down, self-defeating feeling needs to be changed through thinking and actions which generate new feelings of competence.

Perhaps you have developed an exercise program which includes jogging every morning. The morning alarm, clanging like a hook and ladder truck, shatters your slumber much too soon. Your unhappy stomach reminds you of all the cookies you consumed the night before. The thought of jogging sounds about as appealing as stepping into a cold shower with your pajamas on. You would *much* prefer to silence the alarm, snuggle down in the warm, warm covers and catch another thirty minutes of sleep.

Check out your feeling, though. Is it based on sound thinking? Will it result in responsible action? The answer comes back, "No!" So you pull yourself out of bed and dutifully proceed with your exercises. An hour later the feeling has changed. You feel great. You are ready for a productive day. Your old bones tingle with energy and zest. How did that feeling undergo such a transformation? You assumed the responsibility to act on what you knew was best. As a result you feel better—a lot better.

You are responsible for what you do. You can make decisions and live with the consequences of what you decide. If it is a good decision you will feel rewarded. If it is a poor decision, you will sense the let-down and nagging disappointment from short-circuiting what you knew to be best in order to indulge your own temporary comfort and desires.

Some people join religous groups so they won't have to face decisions. They have what one psychologist has called, "decidophobia," a fear of making decisions. By joining a particular religion, a person can look to his or her religious leaders to make decisions. This does not result in happiness, nor productive living. Only as you struggle with decisions and choose to decide on a course of responsible action can you experience growth.

Christianity should be more than a code of conduct—more than a simplistic religious formula which takes personal responsibility away from the individual. Instead, a relationship with Jesus Christ provides special insight into the alternatives to be considered. Some paths in the Christian life will lead to joy and a feeling of achievement. Other paths will lead to remorse and a feeling of frustration. The Bible makes clear what we can anticipate if we take certain paths. As an individual, you decide which way to go, and you gain the benefits or pay the price, depending on which route you've selected.

You may be saying, or at least feeling, "I've read what you've said and it makes sense. But it's so hard and complicated. Isn't there an easier way to get there?" Listen to what the Bible says:

Consider it all joy, my brethren, when you encounter various trials [temptations], knowing that the testing of your faith produces endurance [stedfastness]. And let endurance have its perfect result, that you may be perfect [mature] and complete, lacking in nothing (James 1:2-4).

Pressure can be a hedge—holding you back, hemming you in. That same pressure can be a highway—helping you grow, strengthening your resolve to lean on a Power greater than your own. You'll need all the power you can harness—swimming upstream.

INTERACTION #12

You don't have to go out beating the hedges to find an example of struggle. Growing people are struggling people. As Christians, we need to be sensitive to the process of struggle in those around us.

Check with two of your closest friends. With gentle sincerity, do some probing and find out those areas in which they are experiencing difficulty. In what way can you come alongside and encourage them? Remember not to be judgmental! They need help, not judgment.

Read II Corinthians 1:1-11. From this passage, locate some of the reasons why God allows us to go through times of struggle.

13
Two Helpful Anchors

Circumstance is a rude sort of creature. It never apologizes when it barges in to alter the course of a life. It never knocks before it throws open the front door, strides into the living room and starts to dictate terms. The bother of it all is that you can't get rid of this meddlesome intruder. Like an obnoxious brother-in-law or a football knee, you've got to learn to live with it . . . somehow.

At given times circumstance would like to bully us right off our chosen pathway. Some people bow to this eventuality, meekly allowing the pressure to determine which direction to move. It's an easy cop-out. Circumstance plants itself squarely in the road, gives them a shove and they walk off in the direction of the push . . . just like that.

But is that the only option? Must we always run in the face of our circumstances? Should we ever yield to the tides and undertows that suck backwards at our legs or brashly shove at our backs? Have you ever found yourself looking for a handhold—an anchor, perhaps? Good news. There are two such anchors available. *The first anchor is a well-defined system of values. The second anchor is a set of well-thought-out goals for the future.*

A consciously growing person is one who has the ability to reflect on what he values and to pursue what he cherishes.

What is important to you? What is important from your past? What is priority in your future? You face decisions today . . . tonight. Will they be decisions well anchored in foundational values? Do the decisions you make today help you attain those goals which lead to fulfillment? Only those who recognize the values of the past and the goals of the future will be able to weather the gale force of circumstances without being deterred.

"Hey!" we hear a large segment of the population protest. "What's wrong with yielding to the flow a little?" For them the question has ceased to be, "Is it right or not right?" It has become, "Is it easy or not easy?"

Many have chosen a flexible lifestyle where circumstances determine what is to be done. Quite literally, nothing is sacred. What is right is what is right for you.

The problem with this approach is that there's nothing left to lean on. It's like being on a movie set where every sturdy-looking wall gives way to your weight. The stone is papier-mache. The fine cedar walls are cedar-sprayed plywood. So you can't rest anywhere; you can't depend on anything. Any standard bends if the circumstances warrant a change. Friends can't be counted on. They might not like fulfilling the responsibilities to which they at one time had been committed. It becomes impossible to plan for the future since all you know about it is that it will be different, depending on circumstances.

Coping with change is a blue-chip quality—an extremely useful asset. But cardboard bricks and shifting walls get very weak after a while. Something in the human psyche longs for something solid. We need a foundation of values on which we can depend. Then, when Hurricane Circumstance huffs and puffs and tries to blow us away we can set our anchor firm. We can say with confidence, "On this I can depend. This wall will not wobble. I know what I believe in and what I can count on to be true."

What are values? Remember Brad and Judy a few chapters back? It doesn't take a theologian to detect that fuzzy values make us vulnerable to circumstances. Judy would bitterly agree with that statement. Brad asked her to prove her love for him by "going all the way." In the emotion of such a moment, Judy gave in. She had no clear set of values. Her decision was one of great consequence. The result might have been different if she had earlier taken the time to work through the implications in her heart.

Values are generated from our actions, our knowledge, and our feelings—all three. We *do* what we *know* is right, and we *feel* good because it has communicated to others who we are.

You can't dictate values or legislate them—not really. Values must be *personalized.* It's one thing to be told, "Don't steal." It's another thing to decide not to steal. The second one has been personalized. You have adopted the principle of not stealing into your own family of values. The process of adoption isn't usually a rapid process. Deciding what we will or will not do must be filtered through screens of thought and feeling. And then we test them—try them on.

Untested values look nice on the bookshelf. Leather covers, gold stamping, silk ribbon . . . very impressive. But on the shelf they remain unread, unmarked, unused, unappreciated—and usually unavailable when the howling winds of circumstance descend on our lives.

It's one thing to read a repair manual on how to overhaul a Chevy V-8. You can read it until you fall asleep every night. Underline key passages, star the illustrations, carry it by your side everywhere you go. Far different, however, is the confidence that is gained when you actually slip on your coveralls, grab your wrenches and accomplish what you've studied. It's this experiential knowledge that makes values real and practical as a foundation for growth.

It's the last flight before Tom tries it solo. Soaring confidently with his instructor at three thousand feet, he is thinking how incredibly easy it is to learn to fly. Why didn't he try it years ago? With his background and quick reflexes he is a natural! A sudden mechanical sputter shakes Tom from his reverie. Then . . . silence. The engine is dead. Tom's pulse shoots up as the calm of a few seconds past is replaced with an excited attention.

A quick, furtive glance at the instructor does little to reassure the beginning pilot. He forces himself to screw his mind down on the emergency procedures he had been taught for just such an occasion. He doesn't notice the perspiration on his forehead until it begins to gather in his eyebrows. What next? There . . . there's a field. Looks long enough . . . easy clearance . . . ought to work.

As he begins to guide the silent craft down he wishes he'd listened more closely instead of fantasizing mock dog-fights. If he'd only read more carefully, watched more attentively when the instructor went through the procedures of forced landing without power.

No time for that . . . level with the field now . . . time to set her down . . . . Tom closes his eyes as the wheels plunk and bump through the pasture. As the plane taxies to a stop he leans back and exhales the deep breath he hadn't realized he was holding. It's done. Safely.

At this point the instructor reaches over and flips the ignition switch he'd turned off three thousand feet above the pasture. "Now," he tells his student, "now you really know about landing an airplane after engine failure."

Not all values need to be or can be validated by experience. Those that have been, however, will take on deeper meaning and will be genuinely personalized because they are based on firsthand knowledge.

As we grow, new deposits are added to the bank of values which we've made our own. The more values we have clearly defined, the easier it is to make decisions in the face of confrontations with circumstance.

If the girl in the back seat of the parked car had taken time previously to really think through some of her bookshelf values on marriage and the sanctity of sex, she might have chosen not to be trapped in that predicament.

Steve is offered a new position with his company in a branch office that is just opening up. To accept would mean a promotion, increased salary and some new creative challenges in his work. It would also mean moving his family twelve hundred miles. The kids would have to change schools in midyear. Everyone would have to leave behind old friendships and develop new ones. Finding a new home wouldn't be easy . . .

What should Steve do as he faces this decision? He screens the information through his grid of values in order to plan the best strategy. Getting a good offer means the pressure of circumstance. But it's not the circumstance that will determine Steve's decision. He has a solid basis on which to make his decision, a value grid through which he can sort each bit of information, and then plan the best thing to do. The more you know about what you value, the easier it is to make confident decisions.

The reflection on experiential values forms an anchor from the past which emphasizes what is important to you and develops your character—who you are as a person. The anticipation of what you desire to become is the anchor ahead—the other anchor—which holds you on course.

There are goals to achieve. You struggle through the circumstances, driving forward to attain what you want to do. When you take your eyes off the goals to be achieved or the values of the past, you are in danger of being engulfed by the crashing, sudden waves of circumstance. You are bounced back and forth like a drifting bottle in a restless ocean. In despair you ask, "What's life all about? Where am I headed? What is the purpose of my existence?"

With both anchors firmly fixed it is possible to chart progress. You are moving from a foundation toward a goal. In a real sense you are locked in from both ends. Think of a mountain climb over a steep, slippery terrain with a stiff wind blowing. To insure safety, one climber anchors a rope at the bottom of the cliff. After the first climber scales the height, a rope is secured at the top. Each climber in turn uses the rope to go up the mountain. The climber does so with confidence for he realizes that the rope is secured at both ends. The wind may blow him several yards off the trail, but as long as the climber hangs onto the rope and keeps climbing, there is an assurance that the mountain will be conquered.

DIAGRAM ELEVEN

HELPFUL ANCHORS

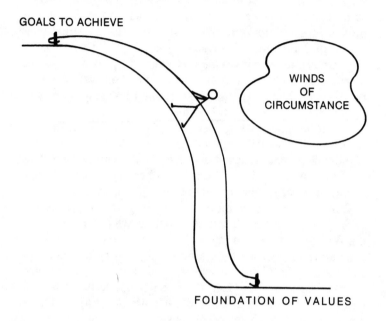

GOALS TO ACHIEVE

WINDS
OF
CIRCUMSTANCE

FOUNDATION OF VALUES

Life that has meaning knows where it's coming from and where it's headed. Circumstances may hamper progress, but they cannot stop you if your anchors are secure.

Do you see the benefit of having these two helpful anchors? Circumstance may deter you, but it will never defeat you, for you know what is important; you know who you are, and you know where you're headed. You're moving in that direction.

One anchor isn't enough. How confident would the mountain climber feel if the rope was fastened only at the base of the cliff? It doesn't matter how securely the rope is tied down, there will be no progress toward the goal until something is nailed down up ahead. A foundation of values will not give purpose to your life until you are directed toward a goal.

One anchor holds you down. *Two anchors free you.* Free you to climb, to explore, to grow. You may know what is important but until you apply that information through a personal value grid, you will grow nowhere. Your journey will appear to be one cul-de-sac after another. You need a strategy to point your nose in a right direction . . . and give the impetus to climb.

Neither is one anchor at the top of the mountain adequate. Goals may be set and goals may be achieved, but until they have been integrated with a core of basic values, the accomplishment will appear futile. Values and goals work together to keep you on course. You will be subjected to the influence of circumstance as everyone else is; but circumstance will not dictate what you do. It will bully you, threaten you, scream loudly in your ears—but you won't be intimidated. Your course is set—the coordinates are locked in. You're free to grow.

It is not uncommon for people to pray that circumstances will be favorable. Students at seminary pray for gifts to come in so they can continue their education without having to take time off to earn money. Blair makes an appointment to see one of his professors and pours out a growing anxiety across the desk. "God must not want me in seminary. I've prayed to Him for money to continue and no money has come in; therefore, God must not want me to continue."

Is it valid to say that circumstance is *always* the message-bearer of God's will? It would be more accurate to characterize circumstance as a vehicle used by God to create in us the proper attitude to fulfill His will. When you and I do God's will, circumstances will fall into place.

Blair's professor asks him, "Was it God's will for you to come to seminary?"

"Yes," he replies.

"Has God given you any reason to feel that He has changed His mind?" This is the critical question.

If Blair says, "Yes, I realize now that a vocational ministry is not what God has for me," you have a solid basis on which to make a decision.

But if the answer comes back, "No, I know God wants me in the ministry," then the key is to remain and to explore ways to generate the necessary financial resources.

You say, "What about Gideon in the Bible? Didn't he determine God's will through circumstances?"

The answer is, "No, God told Gideon what to do. But Gideon lacked faith, so God used a sign to encourage Gideon to believe.

> Then Gideon said to God, "If Thou wilt deliver Israel through me, as Thou hast spoken, behold, I will put a fleece of wool on the threshing floor. If there is dew on the fleece only, and it is dry on all the ground, then I will know that Thou wilt deliver Israel through me, as Thou hast spoken."
>
> And it was so. When he arose early the next morning and squeezed the fleece, he drained the dew from the fleece, a bowl full of water. Then Gideon said to God, "Do not let Thine anger burn against me that I may speak once more; please let me make a test once more with the fleece, let it now be dry only on the fleece, and let there be dew on all the ground."
>
> And God did so that night; for it was dry only on the fleece, and dew was on all the ground (Judges 6:36-40).

God confirmed what He wanted Gideon to do by complying with his request. But notice this important fact: God *did not* use the circumstances to indicate what Gideon was supposed to do. God told Gideon what to do. And when Gideon lacked faith, God confirmed His message because Gideon requested a sign.

God is able to accomplish His purposes in spite of circumstances. He will not be deterred. As those who pray to an all-knowing God, we need to trust His judgment and obey His Word. Circumstances may be used of God in our lives to help us understand His will in a given situation—but not always. Those same circumstances may be used to prove and purify our faith as we proceed from Biblically-based values toward God-honoring goals.

Remember the mountain climbers? We don't let go of our rope because the climb becomes difficult and slippery. On the contrary, we cling even tighter. In the same way, we should cling to our values and grip our goals with new determination when the wind of circumstance would deter us.

Faith doesn't mean backing God into a corner with the request that He arrange circumstances in a way that appears best to our limited vision. Real faith may simply mean sticking with the game plan you've developed in times of prayer, through meditation on truths of Scripture and in counsel with trusted advisors.

Someone has said, "Don't doubt in the darkness what God has shown you in the light."

It is appropriate to ask God for "sticking-it-out power," or to ask Him to make clear anew from the Bible what we should do in any given situation. He will not ask us to do anything He hasn't provided the necessary resources for us to accomplish.

INTERACTION #13

What is important in your life? Be specific. For example, which of the following statements would be most descriptive of you?

_____ 1. I am more comfortable when not involved with other people.

_____ 2. I have several friends I could tell anything to.

_____ 3. People will hurt you if you let them get too close.

_____ 4. It feels good when I have the opportunity to help someone.

_____ 5. It bothers me to have people watch or touch me.

Have you picked one? Which one did you choose? How does that compare with the way you value your relationship with others?

If, on one hand, you claim to need and value the friendship of others, yet you choose numbers one, three, or five, are you being consistent? Number one would indicate a desire to withdraw; number three would indicate a desire to keep others away; number five would indicate a basic distrust of people. Only numbers two (indicating trust) and four (indicating caring) are in harmony with a high value placed on relationships.

Are you ready to try again? What value do you place on money or wealth? Which of the following five statements would you choose?

_____ 1. Money isn't important as long as I've got enough to live on.

_____ 2. Opportunity in life comes to the wealthy.

_____ 3. I would prefer to go on welfare than to take some jobs.

_____ 4. The world owes me a living.

_____ 5. Most important to me are an interesting job and a good income.

Number one would indicate wealth is valued only as a means of maintenance. Numbers three and four would be indication of attitudes of non-productivity or destitution. Choice of number two or five would indicate a high value placed on abundance or productivity.

In examining your values, you need to determine if what you practice is consistent with what you claim to value. Is it consistent to:

a. value moral integrity, yet cheat on your taxes when you think you won't get caught?

b. claim that you respect and esteem others when you find it hard to mix with people who are different?

c. purport to be open with people, yet in practice keep them guessing?

d. resist coercion, yet give your child candy if he or she promises to be good?

e. feel you are well adjusted even though your appetite is sometimes gone and you can't sleep well?

f.   recognize how important it is for each person to contribute to a worthwhile project, yet refuse to get involved unless the task is interesting?

How does what you claim to value match up with the way you live? Perhaps the following activity will help you to answer that question.

Make a list of the ten most important people in your life. Add to that list the ten activities you feel are most important and the ten things you cherish most. After completing the thirty items, put the list away. Keep a journal of your activities for the next two weeks. Then compare your list of values with your record of activities. Do your activities validate your values?

A key to successful living is to know what you value and to live accordingly. As you plan for the future, lock into those values that are carried out in the way you live. Learn how to add activities to your schedule which will enhance your values and to delete from your life those things which will detract.

What is important? Where are you headed? As you clarify and enlarge the answers to these two questions, life takes on a new perspective. You stand prepared to take charge of your own decisions, and to move one step upstream.

14
Making Decisions

A story is told of a man who approached a farmer asking for work in return for some food. The farmer gave the man some wood to split. It was only a short time later that the hired man returned with his task accomplished. The farmer was impressed. After the meal, the farmer invited the man to stay and complete additional work for him. A wage was agreed upon and the man started in stacking the wood he had just split. Again the job was done quickly and neatly. Each task the farmer assigned to the man was completed with diligence and dispatch. The farmer was delighted he had located such good help.

Because his new hand had been working so hard, the farmer decided to give him an easier task. He took the man to the potato bin and asked him to sort the potatoes into three piles—small, medium, and large. He picked a sample of each size to get the man started, then left him to accomplish the task.

Lunch hour came and the hired man failed to show up. The farmer was surprised for he had expected the job to be finished long ago. After lunch, he went to the potato cellar to see what had happened. The man was sitting despondently on the cellar floor with one potato in each pile, the one the farmer had put there.

"What's wrong?" the farmer inquired. "Why haven't you finished this job?"

"Work I can do," the man replied, "but these decisions are killing me."

The world is looking for skillful decision-makers. One of the most important skills a person can ever possess is the ability to make good decisions. One decision can alter the course of a life forever—or the course of history. And some decisions are so agonizingly difficult. How does one know which decision is the right one?

Ken just graduated from high school. Should he go on to college? He's not sure what he should take if he does seek further schooling. He's not sure what kind of work he wants. Maybe he should get a job pumping gas for a while until he determines what he wants to do. Then there's always the Army. . . . He's been dating Wilma for two years. He likes her a lot. Should he ask Wilma to marry him? How would he support a family? The decisions Ken makes will affect the rest of his life. Flipping a coin wouldn't be right. The implications of the various options are too heavy—too permanent.

Jean announces to her parents that she is going to marry Greg. Having already set the date, she very much wants her parents' blessing and support. The parents are devout Christians. They feel badly that Greg is of another faith. But loving their daughter deeply, they long to reassure Jean and support her in her wedding plans. Still, they are firmly convinced that her marriage to Greg would be a mistake she will bitterly regret in later years. Jean must make up her own mind, but her parents are reluctant to compromise strongly-felt principles. What should they do? They do not want to alienate their daughter, but they don't want to ignore principles either.

Some decisions demand to be faced when we seem least able to confront them. A couple has lived together for more than fifty years. Their marriage has had great joy. Each partner has found reward in doing things together. A sudden illness comes and the husband dies. The wife wishes she could die, too. What new activities can she find at her age to soothe the ache of loneliness and the recurring bouts with grief and self-pity?

This chapter suggests a process for decision-making. Each person employing the process should be able to determine the best alternative for a given time. The alternative chosen is really secondary to the process, for it is the process of making decisions that leads to growth and maturity.

DIAGRAM TWELVE

DECISION-MAKING PROCESS

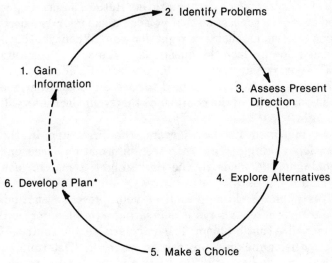

*Plan requires:

A. Specified time
B. Schedule
C. Relational accountability

Growth implies making decisions, trying something you haven't tried before. Careful examination based on sound thinking and worthy feelings leads you to make a choice.

You will not succeed, however, unless you follow up the choice with a plan for implementation. When stress comes along, you will fail and go back to your old ways. That's when your friend comes alongside to encourage you. The plan is reinstated and you have learned the process of growth.

149

If you thumbed to this chapter first looking for easy answers . . . sorry. It won't happen here. We should learn to avoid those who crank out easy answers to difficult situations. Keep seeking out that sort of counsel and it becomes doubtful that you will learn how to cope with the questions of life. Every time you have a problem you will need to go back to some "guru" for another answer.

This chapter is not guru-approved. Rather, it encourages you to learn a process so that you can make your own decisions—decisions that are right for you. When you have learned how to face the questions of life and to come up with your own answers, you have attained a good level of maturity. You will be enabled to face difficult situations head-on, and have the confidence that your decisions will be right.

As indicated in the diagram, the first step in the decision-making process is to seek information. Decisions should not be made in the dark. Light a match; look around.

Next, take a close-up look at your present situation. Determine in what ways it is creating a problem for you. Personalize that problem. The only variable you control in the decision-making process is yourself. Determining where you are having difficulty is a giant step toward exploring an alternative for change.

The third step is simply to ask yourself: "What am I doing now and where will that ultimately take me?" You may resist asking yourself these sorts of questions, but if you really tackle them the result can be revealing. Oftentimes they will spotlight the futility of your present activities.

Either through counsel or on your own initiative, consider what alternatives are available to you. Here is an opportunity to exercise creativity that may pay rich dividends. For each alternative, try to think through possible problems should you choose that alternative. Also, try to think through what the result might be.

Step five is to make a choice. This is the action step. It

may be that you choose to continue what you have been doing. You may choose one of the alternatives that you explored.

You may sincerely desire to grow and to change but may fail in your efforts because you stop with step five. When the pressure hits, your new choice goes out the window and you revert to a habitual response which has been used many times before. When this happens, you become discouraged at your apparent inability to change. You reconcile yourself to mediocrity or destructive habits simply because you haven't taken the process far enough.

Change *can* occur, but it requires a well-developed plan. At least three ingredients should be included in the plan. How long are you going to try what it is you have chosen to do? Short periods of time are better than longer periods, for it provides greater opportunity for assessment and adjustment. Next, you should ask, "What are the sequential steps involved in implementing the plan?" What needs to be done first? Then what? And so on.

The third ingredient in the plan has been called relational accountability. It could also be called the buddy system. With whom are you going to share your plan? Who will help you stick with it? Chances are, since you're human, you will fall short on at least part of what you set out to accomplish. That first failure is a very sensitive and crucial moment. The path is littered with abandoned plans following initial failures. At this vital moment you need a special someone to come alongside, help you pick up the pieces and encourage you to get started back on the plan once again.

Now that you've looked at the diagram and read over the steps, put your knowledge to work in the following specific situation. Nancy comes to you and requests help to make some decisions. As you try to gain information, you learn the following:

Nancy has been married to Neil for ten years. Neil is an alcoholic who does most of his drinking while at work. Nancy is concerned because Neil is a truckdriver and she feels he could kill someone by drinking on the job. She admits that she inquires often as to whether he drank that day, and she nags him when he admits to drinking.

Neil and Nancy do not have children. A major turning point in their lives seemed to have occurred when Nancy miscarried in the third year of their marriage. Neil and Nancy were both extremely shaken by the miscarriage but reacted in different ways. Neil began to drink heavily. Nancy, in her search for meaning, became a Christian. Her husband has shown no interest in Christianity.

Despite her new faith, Nancy has lost ground in several areas during the past two years. She has gained weight, seldom prepares a good meal or cleans the house. Involved in few activities, Nancy finds plenty of time to talk on the phone to a few ladies in the church. Most of their conversations center on Neil's behavior and how unfortunate it is that Nancy has to "bear this burden."

There it is—a real life situation in desperate need of the decision-making process. You have enough information to move on to the next step. How are you going to help Nancy identify the problem? Be careful. Remember, you're not talking to Neil. You're talking to Nancy. Neil's drinking is not *her* problem. That may be Neil's problem, but it isn't Nancy's.

The problem is that Nancy is miserable. She is not involved in constructive activities and she has lost a sense of pride in her personal appearance. Nancy is unhappy and that is the problem.

Resist the temptation to moralize—don't be too quick to give rapid-fire answers. Remember the process of struggle in making your own decisions is very important. Nancy doesn't need a shoot-from-the-hip cure-all. She doesn't need to hear a catalog reading of Scriptural references. Nancy needs to be encouraged to work through the process of decision-making. What she needs from you is support and interest as you urge her to follow through each step along the way.

As you help Nancy to assess the present direction, you might ask questions such as, "What do you think it accomplishes when you nag Neil about drinking on the job? Where will that ultimately lead?" As Nancy thinks through this question carefully, she begins to see that her tactics have been nonproductive. Neil continues to drink. If anything, he's drinking more now than he used to. The nagging is actually driving a deep wedge between them. Neil withdraws and doesn't want to talk. Nancy finds herself with greater frustration than before she started nagging for she has accomplished nothing worthwhile.

Other questions and insights follow. "What has been gained by letting personal habits of grooming go? How has gossiping with other ladies in the church helped or hindered you? What has been achieved by your inability to get involved in any projects?"

What can Nancy do? Don't leave her with the broken pieces of her past futilities. Her first option is to keep on doing what she is doing now. Where would that lead?

Some alternatives may have negative consequences. She might consider killing herself. Once again, it is necessary to ask, "What would that resolve?" Another alternative would be to start drinking with Neil. A third alternative might involve seeking a separation or divorce.

Nancy finally decides the right thing for her to do is to begin a program of self-improvement. She decides to lose weight, get her hair fixed, start cooking balanced meals, clean the house, get involved in a project helping some needy people in the church and quit nagging Neil. It is Nancy's plan. No one dictated it to her or legislated it for her. She thought through the alternatives and chose a path.

The decision makes sense and appears to be headed in a positive direction. All that remains is to develop a plan.

"How long do you want to stay on the new program?" you ask Nancy.

"For a year," Nancy replies.

Don't buy it! That's too long. Two weeks is a more logical limit. After that period the whole decision-making process should be worked through once again.

The more specific Nancy can make elements of her two-week schedule the better chance it will have of survival. A vague general plan tends to conform to one's worst habits. So Nancy develops detailed menus for each evening meal during the two-week period. She determines a time for an appointment with the hairdresser and writes it down on the calendar. She selects music for each evening to insure a pleasant atmosphere in her home. She decides what to wear each day, so that she will be attractive. Working out a diet, Nancy sets a realistic weight-loss goal for the two weeks. She determines a time to contact the church and volunteer her services for a special project.

Most important, Nancy needs that special friend who will provide her with relational accountability. Feeling that the pastor's wife understands her better than anyone else, Nancy asks her for help as she launches out on her plan. At last the schedule is completed. Nancy has decided to start next Monday and try the plan for two weeks.

Monday, Tuesday, and Wednesday go well. Nancy is feeling the thrill of accomplishment. Thursday starts out okay, but unexpected company drops in for an hour in the afternoon. Behind schedule, Nancy realizes that she will really have to rush to prepare the roast beef she has planned for that evening. The pressure knifes in and gives her a severe headache. While she browns the roast the phone rings and the roast is overcooked. And where's Neil? He's an hour late. Finally he comes in the door—drunk. He tosses his dirty jacket on a chair, spoiling the effect of her freshly-cleaned house.

Suddenly Nancy's good intentions are lost. She turns on Neil and blurts out, "You don't love me! Here I've slaved all day just to make the house nice for you. I cook a good meal and what do you do? You come home an hour late and you're drunk."

After a few brief unpleasant exchanges, Nancy runs crying into her bedroom and slams the door. Neil leaves to visit the local tavern.

Nancy is still weeping on her bed an hour later when the phone rings. It's the pastor's wife. "How's it going?" she asks cheerily.

"Terrible!" Nancy chokes her reply. "I just blew it. I destroyed everything I worked on all week in five minutes tonight."

The pastor's wife listens while Nancy recounts the events of the day. In a kind, non-judgmental way she encourages Nancy. "Well, Friday's a new day. What have you got planned?" she inquires.

Nancy is back on her plan. The vital element of relational accountability saves another plan from the scrap heap of New Year's resolutions and good intentions.

Decision-making is more than a handy six-step plan. It's life. No one ever maintains status quo. If you're not forging forward, you're deteriorating, slipping backwards, however subtly or imperceptibly that may occur. Real life means growth and growth is always against the current. Drifting backwards is as easy as letting go, as easy as giving up, and has about it the flavor of death.

Making progress—taking charge—in any area of life requires a plan. Decision-making is what moving upstream is all about.

INTERACTION #14

What decisions do you face?

The process described in the last few pages may embrace any number of problematic situations. Perhaps you've found yourself asking one or more of the following questions:

— I feel like I'm drifting from my kids. How can I get to know them better?

— I've forgotten what it's like to spend time with God. Where do I find the time to pray?

— My sister and I don't communicate anymore. Resentment is really building up in me. What can I do to get close to her again?

— I'm feeling dull and listless and I know I need to get on an exercise program. But I can never stick with it. How do I really get into it?

— My job seems to have dead-ended and I'm getting more discouraged with it every day. Should I quit and find something else—perhaps go back to school for some more training?

Maybe you can't identify with any of these questions. You could easily insert your own. Everyone faces difficult decisions moving through daily living. Not all decisions are as complicated as those faced by Nancy in our illustration. But any decision, large or small, simple or complex, can be processed through the six steps described in this chapter. Ask a friend to help you work through the steps in your problem situation. Become an effective decision-maker. The growth that leads to maturity comes when we make decisions and live with the consequences of what we decide.

15
One Step At a Time

There's nothing like growing to help a person grow. Double talk? Not really. The young wife who has struggled to develop a savings program may find it easier to come up with a winning, working physical exercise plan. The father who has plotted a careful course to build communication bridges to his children may find he has an easier time planning and implementing a personal reading program.

Aren't these things unrelated? No, not if they're all a part of *you*. The person who has learned to grow through struggle and sheer determination in one area of life isn't likely to forget that knowledge when he's nose to nose with another wall. The more you grow the greater your capacity to grow. It's contagious, infectious and thoroughly worth the price of the disease, remembering that the alternative is *stagnation*.

Planned, step-by-step growth is nothing new. Farmers wait for it; economists chart it; athletes train for it; engineers diagram it; scientists eyeball it in a thousand test tubes. And chances are they all go home at night kicking themselves because they can't lose weight or they never have time to make improvements in their backyard. There's nothing novel or unique about principles of growth. It's just that most people don't apply what they know to where they live.

Once you've had the immense pleasure of watching yourself grow out of an area of nagging defeat and habitual mediocrity, you'll want to attack new lairs of discouragement. Personal roadblocks will never look quite so immovable again!

In 1968, Dave and Luci Mai lived in our home. It was the final year in their preparation to go to Nairobi as missionaries. I should have anticipated the dangers of housing an ex-basketball coach under our roof, but I hadn't. His not-so-subtle suggestion that I start a jogging program posthaste caught me totally off guard.

Sure, I was thirty-four and overweight. True, my energy level had a tendency to droop and sag a little by mid-afternoon. But jogging? Aw, c'mon, coach.

Dave was smilingly persistent.

"Just try it, Gordon. Try three days a week—a half hour a shot—see what kind of difference it makes."

Dave could have easily run circles and figure-eights around me as I wheezed along the Oregon country lanes. Day after day, week after week, he persistently invited me to run with him. I was almost glad when Dave and Luci finally sailed for Nairobi. Now perhaps I would recover from the periodic attacks of bad conscience when I skipped a jogging session in favor of an extra hour of sack time.

I always felt better when I ran. But the discipline of it sounded fanatical—or worse yet, habit-forming. For the next six years I was a sunshine athlete, emerging when the weather looked inviting. (Living in western Oregon, I was pretty safe.)

Two years ago, however, my conscience suffered a massive relapse, taking a sudden turn for the worse. I was teaching a class to seminary students and one of the young men presented a paper on physical exercise. Holding up an old section of drainpipe encrusted with the rust of ages, the student bade us think of the interior lining of our own veins and arteries. The rest of his address on the clogging effects of cholesterol was lost to me. How had he done it—all the way from Nairobi? The coach had struck again.

Ultimately I would pay a price for ignoring and abusing my body. I would not enjoy the quality of life that would be possible if I started a consistent exercise program. So I went home and developed a plan. Each morning I started out running. Six months later I added five basic exercises. Moving ever so gradually, but at least consistently, I increased the number of repetitions for each exercise to a maintenance level.

And I'm maintaining! Besides that, I'm twenty-five pounds lighter. Not that it's stopped raining on early Oregon mornings. It's still not easy on those dark, wet days to tread out into the elements and run my route. But I do! It's gaining me an extra hour of productive work every day and, as my energy level has gone up, so has my enjoyment of life. Whatever I do, I feel more like really getting in and *doing* it. Dave, wherever you are, I'm glad you heckled me so unmercifully. Now I can't afford to quit.

But growth leads to growth. And you hold the evidence in your hands. For a number of years I wanted to write a book, but getting started was . . . well, you know. Then Larry and I developed a plan. With the confidence of one working program under my belt, my reservoir of self-esteem allowed me to attempt another. So we sketched out a game plan, roughed a schedule, did a little dreaming, then hauled out those blank, blank pieces of paper.

Transcribing our first few discussions to get an overview, we took our notes to a cabin in the woods or up to a mountain for a number of successive Saturdays. We gave ourselves to the writing. Progress was evaluated along the way and more than once we had to revise an overly-optimistic schedule.

But now the work is complete. And I've grown. Sure it's risky. I could have failed, or dead-ended, or bogged down in the middle. But I'm happy I endured the setbacks and disappointments to stay with the plan. Without that plan and without the encouragement from Larry, I would have become discouraged along the way and tossed the idea into the junk pile of famous first chapters and great expectations.

Maybe you have such a junk pile in the back corner of your life. You've tried and failed once too often and now you're ready to settle down to a second-class, grade B, ho-hum sort of sojourn on Planet Earth. Wait! Don't sign anything yet! You can grow through your struggles. The process will be anything but easy, yet the prospects will be anything but small.

Each winter my son Mark and I face the task of pruning our filbert orchard. Invariably, pruning time comes at the worst time of year. When it rains, the water runs down your arms and neck. You dream about the warm house, the football games on television, the fireplace. It can really be miserable out there pruning trees.

But we do it because we want a good crop the next fall. We stick with our plan and prune the trees to stimulate new growth and encourage greater productivity.

Come to think of it, that's what I want in my life. Did I hear a whispered "Amen" to that? Start by taking charge. Move one step upstream.

You may find it less tiring than treading water. And a whole lot more rewarding.